ALBUCASIS
(ABU AL-QASIM) (AL-ZAHRAWI)

Renowned Muslim Surgeon
of the Tenth Century

Great Muslim Philosophers and Scientists of the Middle Ages™

ALBUCASIS
(ABU AL-QASIM)
(AL-ZAHRAWI)

Renowned Muslim Surgeon
of the Tenth Century

Fred Ramen

The Rosen Publishing Group, Inc., New York

For my aunt, Barbara

Published in 2006 by The Rosen Publishing Group, Inc.
29 East 21st Street, New York, NY 10010

First Edition

Library of Congress Cataloging-in-Publication Data

Ramen, Fred.
Albucasis (Abu al-Qasim al-Zahrawi): renowned Muslim surgeon of the Tenth Century/Fred Ramen.
    p. cm.—(Great Muslim philosophers and scientists of the Middle Ages)
Includes bibliographical references and index.
ISBN 1-4042-0510-1 (lib. bdg.)
1. Abu al-Qasim Khalaf ibn 'Abbas al-Zahrawi, d. 1013?
2. Physicians—Arab countries—Biography. 3. Surgeons—Arab countries—
Biography. 4. Physicians—Spain—Biography. 5. Surgeons—Spain—
Biography. 6. Medicine, Arab—Spain—History. 7. Medicine,
Medieval—Spain.
I. Title. II. Series.

R144.A2R36 2006
610'.92—dc22

                                                    2005015786

Manufactured in the United States of America

On the cover: Artist Ernest Board painted this image of Albucasis as he would have appeared in a Muslim hospital in Córdoba, Spain, around AD 1000.

CONTENTS

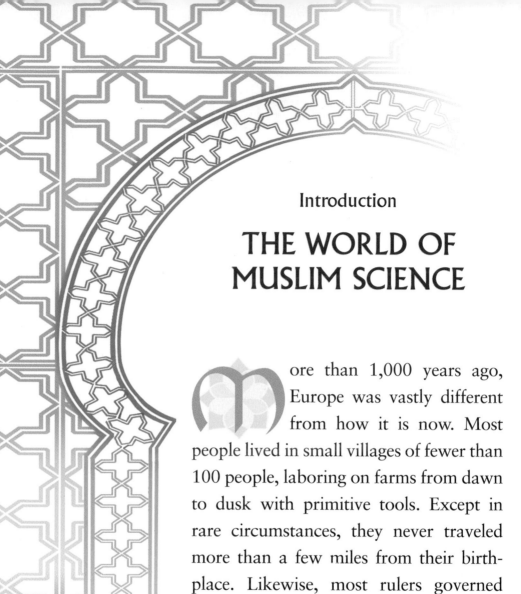

Introduction

THE WORLD OF MUSLIM SCIENCE

ore than 1,000 years ago, Europe was vastly different from how it is now. Most people lived in small villages of fewer than 100 people, laboring on farms from dawn to dusk with primitive tools. Except in rare circumstances, they never traveled more than a few miles from their birthplace. Likewise, most rulers governed little more than the area in which they could travel by horseback in a single day. Gone was the unity of the Roman Empire, when Europe south of the Alps and west of the Rhine had been a single

The Isidorean *mappa mundi* (map of the world) was created in the eleventh century. Asia can be seen at the top half of the map, while Europe is featured at the bottom left and Africa at the bottom right.

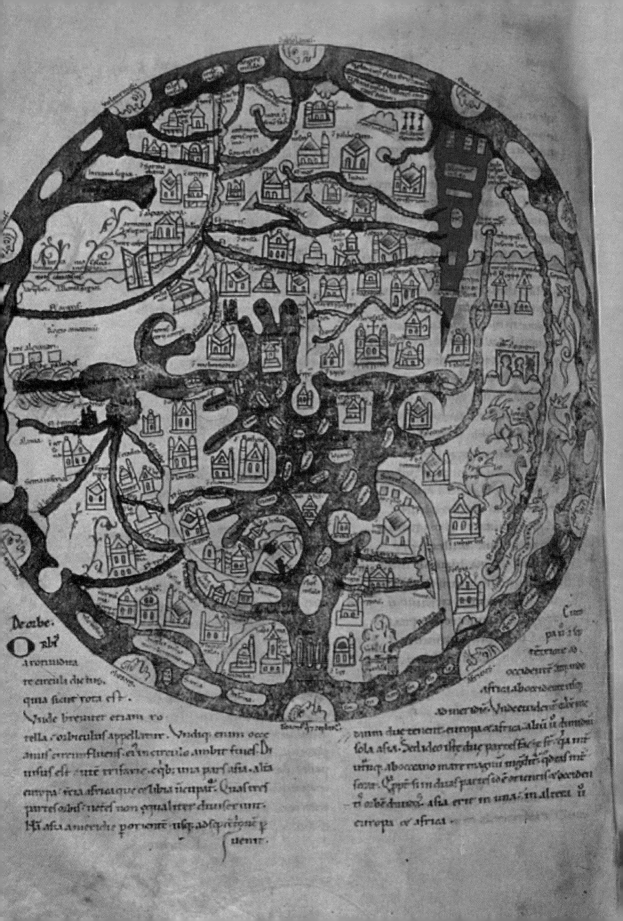

political entity. Before the Roman Empire collapsed into a hundred years of invasion and civil war, it had produced the longest period of peace and prosperity in European history.

Little survived the fall of the Roman Empire besides its extensive system of roads and the Christian church, the last truly continent-wide institution. But even the church was divided against itself; the schism that would permanently separate its Eastern (Orthodox) and Western (Catholic) branches was already a fact of everyday life. The attempt to find a single ruler powerful enough to restore the Roman Empire was eventually found in Charlemagne (742–814), first ruler of the Holy Roman Empire, beginning in AD 768. Charlemagne's leadership had only produced an unhappy marriage of Germany and Italy, where jealous noblemen in both kingdoms allied themselves with the pope or the emperor out of personal greed and ambition. Any attempts made to cure the corruption and failure of much of the clergy had failed under the reforms of Pope Gregory VII (1020–1085). These changes would soon set the pope against the emperor in a struggle for control of the church.

Europe was hardly as backward and primitive as the term "Dark Ages" (the name once used for the period between the ultimate fall of the Roman Empire in AD 476 and about AD 1000) implies. However, it is a fact that much of the impressive learning of the ancient world was forgotten during that era. At the time, Latin, the language of the

Frumentum.

al. natuie. c. q. h. i. z. melius ereo. pingue ponerosiz. Iuuamentu aperit apostemata. nocumentu facit opplationes. remono noci. cum bene peratur.

This illustration is from a fourteenth-century translation of *Tableau of Health*, a manuscript written between AD 1052 and AD 1063 by Ibn Botlán, a Christian physician from Baghdad. The health manual is known in the West as *Tacuinum Sanitatis*. In more than 280 separate articles, it describes various plants and their beneficial effects on a person's health, as well as theories about proper breathing, exercising, and eating. Historians believe that Albucasis consulted this manuscript and even annotated a copy of it in his lifetime, elements of which were included in later translations.

Roman Empire, was known only to a few people, most of them clergymen. Even fewer people could understand Greek except for those living in the Byzantine Empire, so knowledge of the great works of philosophers such as Plato (428–348 BC) and Aristotle (384–322 BC) was extremely limited. Medicine was a lost art in Europe; disease killed many people before they turned twenty, and surgery was almost always fatal.

Yet there were still parts of Europe where the hoard of knowledge accumulated by the Greeks and Romans remained vital. Just over the Pyrenees mountains from France, on the Iberian Peninsula, in a land called al-Andalus by its Muslim conquerors but known to us as a region of Spain, ancient works were being studied and translated into Arabic. In al-Andalus, the practice of medicine was a vital art. Muslim doctors in al-Andalus achieved a level of learning not seen in Europe until the end of the Renaissance, nearly 500 years later. From this colony of learning would come the greatest physician of his age, Abu al-Qasim al-Zahrawi (AD 936–1013), known to the Western world as Albucasis. Among the many Muslim physicians and scientists who advanced medical science in their lifetimes, Albucasis would codify the art of surgery in an encyclopedic work that is still read today, *The Method (Al-Tasrif)*. His story is intimately connected to the history of Islam and how Muslims preserved and added to the knowledge of the old Roman world, information that Europe would not discover for another 400 years.

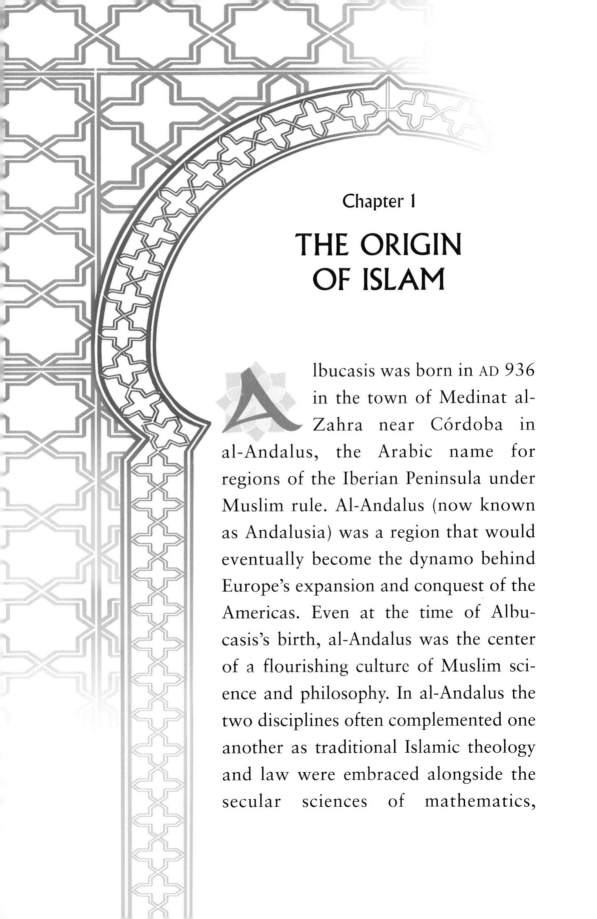

Chapter 1

THE ORIGIN
OF ISLAM

lbucasis was born in AD 936 in the town of Medinat al-Zahra near Córdoba in al-Andalus, the Arabic name for regions of the Iberian Peninsula under Muslim rule. Al-Andalus (now known as Andalusia) was a region that would eventually become the dynamo behind Europe's expansion and conquest of the Americas. Even at the time of Albucasis's birth, al-Andalus was the center of a flourishing culture of Muslim science and philosophy. In al-Andalus the two disciplines often complemented one another as traditional Islamic theology and law were embraced alongside the secular sciences of mathematics,

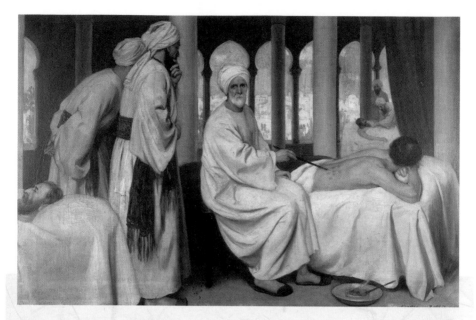

In this oil painting from 1912, artist Ernest Board rendered Albucasis as he would have tended to a patient in the hospital at Córdoba, Spain, around AD 1000. In this image, two doctors watch closely as Albucasis "blisters" the lower back of one of his patients. Blistering, or bloodletting, was a common practice in Spain and throughout Europe in Albucasis's lifetime. Physicians believed that the procedure promoted healing by helping rid the body of toxins.

physics, anatomy, biology, chemistry, and astronomy. Albucasis was a Muslim living in the most powerful Muslim region west of Baghdad (the chief city in the Muslim world and home to the successors of the prophet Muhammad). To understand how Europe would be dominated by Muslims for the better part of a millennium, and the effect that Islam and Arabic culture would have in shaping its future, we must first explore the history of the Mediterranean region. This section of the world represented a crossroads of two continents. The Mediterranean was the basin of European civilization for more than 5,000 years.

EARLY CIVILIZATIONS

Ever since the first empires of Mesopotamia extended themselves to the shores of the Mediterranean, the people living in this region have communicated, fought, and shared knowledge with one another.

The first cities appeared in Mesopotamia (present-day Iraq) in about 5000 BC. Here, for the first time, agriculture made it possible for thousands of people to live close to each other. The goals and advancements of these new societies remain the basis of civilization throughout the world: writing to preserve records; mathematics to manage supplies; and codes of laws to govern people. In time, the cities combined first into kingdoms and then empires, warring against each other for control of the Fertile Crescent, the arable region between the Tigris and Euphrates rivers.

Soon other cultures had founded their own civilizations. The first to border directly on the Mediterranean was Egypt, where impressive monuments and artworks still offer a glimpse of the power and grandeur of one of the greatest empires of the ancient world. However, Egypt remained somewhat isolated and mostly uninterested in extending itself much beyond the lands that border the Nile River. It was another group, the Persians, who inhabited the region now occupied by Iran, who first burst into prominence in the region. The Persians ultimately conquered Mesopotamia and extended Persia into Asia Minor (present-day Turkey).

The Persians were accomplished conquerors, and their continuing expansion of Persia brought them into conflict with the Greeks, inhabitants of the mountainous Balkan Peninsula. Always a fractious and divided people, the Greeks were great merchants. They traded with all the civilizations of the Mediterranean, and from them took their best ideas. The Greeks borrowed writing from the Phoenicians, artistic techniques from the Egyptians, and mathematics from the Babylonians. They incorporated these disciplines into their own unique Greek culture, improving them as they did so. Two invasions by the Persians ended in Greek victories, ushering in a great period of expansion and learning. Greek colonies

This is a detail of a relief carving in the ancient Persian city of Persepolis. The Persians were great conquerors. They could not, however, suppress the rise of the Greeks, whose armies conquered Persia and ended the expansion of its empire around 480 BC. Persians were able to sustain their leadership in parts of the region for more than a century, however, until they were completely overthrown by Greek armies led by Alexander the Great in 330 BC.

spread throughout the Mediterranean, to what are now Sicily and Italy, and even the future site of Marseille in France. During this period, Greek philosophy and learning flourished in the doctrines of Socrates (470–399 BC), Plato, and Aristotle.

THE MACEDONIAN EMPIRE

Eventually, the division between the various Greek city-states would be their downfall, even as the extraordinary ideas of Greek culture, known as Hellenism, continued to expand to the rest of the world. North of Greece, in a region called Macedonia, a warrior king named Philip (359–336 BC) trained a new army based upon an improvement on traditional Greek fighting methods. He then used these methods to conquer all of Greece. But rather than destroy Greek culture, Philip wanted to absorb it; he hired the philosopher Aristotle to be the tutor for his young son Alexander (356–323 BC). After Philip's death by assassination, Alexander took an army of Macedonians and Greeks on the most impressive invasion in history. With his fierce army, Alexander struck into Asia Minor, defeated and crushed the Persians, swept through Egypt and Mesopotamia, and reached the outskirts of India before his weary soldiers forced him to turn back. These invasions forged an enormous empire.

Alexander did not live long enough to secure his Macedonian Empire, which collapsed almost immediately

This manuscript illustration describes the medicinal properties of plants and features the Greek philosopher Aristotle teaching Alexander the Great. Based on the writings of one of the most prominent physicians of the Abbasid dynasty, Yuhanna ibn Bukhtishu, the manuscript shows how the Greeks influenced Muslim medicine. The Abbasids produced Muslim hospitals that served both the wealthy and the poor. Muslim physicians treated tumors and performed surgery and could distinguish between measles and smallpox.

This sixth-century bronze lion was found in Germany. At its height in 323 BC, the Macedonian Empire had absorbed Persia and had control over lands as far as India. Highly influential, Greek culture had a tremendous impact on Muslim medicine. Educated Muslims often translated Greek manuscripts into Arabic, preserving the knowledge for future generations.

after his death from disease in 323 BC. The greatest impact of Macedonia, however, was the spread of Greek culture, language, and learning throughout the Persian and Egyptian empires that Alexander had conquered. Egypt would be ruled by Greeks until the time of the Roman Empire, as would large portions of the Persian Empire. Greek became the standard language of the eastern Mediterranean, even after the later Roman conquests.

THE ROMAN EMPIRE

It was the Romans who next strode onto the stage of the Mediterranean world. Like the Greeks, they were geniuses at incorporating the best of the cultures they encountered into their own society; but unlike the Greeks, they had an excellence for organization and governing. From a single insignificant village in the middle of Italy (founded, according to legend, in 753 BC), by about 150 BC they had defeated all rivals for dominance in the Mediterranean and had conquered Greece itself. While it was Alexander and the Macedonians who spread Greek culture to the east, it was the Romans who spread it to the west. Greek philosophy, poetry, and literature forged the foundation of Roman thought, profoundly influencing all aspects of their society. However, even with their genius for government, the Romans could not solve the problems that were splitting their empire apart. After two centuries of peace, civil war and invasions by Germanic peoples from beyond the Rhine ultimately caused the collapse of the empire, and the last Roman emperor was killed in battle in AD 476.

The eastern half of the Roman Empire, however, survived. It is usually referred to as the Byzantine Empire after the fall of Rome because the original name of its capital, Constantinople, was Byzantium. The Byzantine Empire was largely Roman in name only because it remained isolated from western Europe and its language was Greek, not Latin. For centuries, however, the Byzantine Empire preserved the glory of the Greco-Roman civilization, although it was ultimately unable to revive it. Much of its history would instead be spent in defending itself against invasions from the east, especially from the Persians.

In the midst of this clash of empires, city-dwelling and nomadic Arabs, or Bedouin, lived a traditional existence on

Arab armies descend on Constantinople, the wealthy capital of the Byzantine Empire, in this page from the *Scylitzes Chronicle* written by eleventh-century historian John Scylitzes. Although Byzantine Greeks defended themselves against the Arabs (first in 717 and again in 726) using the unique "Greek fire" technique, the city was eventually occupied in 1204 by Christian crusaders. Greek fire was a petroleum-based mixture that, when launched from tubes mounted on Greek ships, would cause nearly inextinguishable fires.

the Arabian Peninsula. Well-situated to conduct trade between Europe and Asia, the Arabs controlled the caravan routes from Syria to India and China, and sailed ships up and down the Red Sea and the Persian Gulf. At various times they had been under the leadership of the Persian, Roman, and Byzantine empires, but at the end of the sixth century, war between Persia and Byzantium left them as they normally were—under no outside dominion and with no formal political structure. It would take the creation of a new religion, Islam, to unite the peoples of the peninsula.

THE EMERGENCE OF ISLAM

The prophet Muhammad (AD 570–632) was born in the city of Mecca (also known as Makkah), an important trading center in Arabia. As a young man, he traveled widely into Syria on trading missions and became an accomplished merchant. He married Khadija, a wealthy widow in 596. She bore him five children: four daughters and a son, who died in infancy.

Muhammad was an intelligent man who liked to meditate and pray alone in a cave near Mecca. In 610, while meditating, he had a vision of the angel Gabriel, who spoke to him. This was the first of several revelations that would form the basis of the Qur'an (also known as the Koran), the sacred holy book of the Muslims.

Over time, the revelations Muhammad received led him to proclaim Islam, a new religion that was different from the idol worship then practiced by the Arabs of Mecca. Like Judaism and Christianity, Islam was and is a monotheistic religion, meaning that its followers believed in only one god instead of the many idols worshipped at the Kaaba, the black, rectangular temple in Mecca believed to have been created by Abraham. Muhammad also incorporated many of the traditions of Judaism and Christianity, proclaiming that he had received the final revelation of God that completed the prior revelations to Jews and Christians.

At first, Muhammad had only one follower, his wife Khadija; soon his cousin Ali converted to Islam, and then his close friend Abu Bakr. Others converted in secret and later Muhammad began to preach publicly in 613. Most people did not heed Muhammad's message, though he managed to gain enough followers to alarm the rulers of Mecca. Much of the wealth of these leaders was based not only on their central location at the crossroads of many of

The birthplaces of the prophet Muhammad and his followers Ali, Abu Bakr, and Muhammad's daughter Fatima are illustrated in this painting taken from a seventeenth-century Persian manuscript. After the Prophet's death in 632, Islam spread rapidly, gaining converts throughout Arabia. Within a century, Islam made its way throughout the entire Persian Empire, west across North Africa to Spain, and east across central Asia to India.

شتری از زهره و تمس و قمر

چپس و قمر

بود فرامشان همه باید کر

بهر سبزین کوی نشیا فراز

بود خوابشکر آن بهره نار

مولود حضرت

مولود حضرت علی

دکان حضرت صدیق رضی الله عنه

مولود حضرت فاطم

حجره مظلم

ش کن از من صفت در دعا

را کر احمد بن الشودا انج و عا

بهر دعا کرده نوقت رسول

بهر آن راه بوقت وصول

The Five Pillars of Islam

At the heart of Islam are the Five Pillars, the most fundamental beliefs that every Muslim shares. They are:

1. **Belief in one God** *(Shahadah)*: Muslims are expected to profess their faith daily in this simple prayer: "There is no god but God (Allah), and Muhammad is his prophet."

2. **Prayer** *(Salah)*: Muslims are expected to recite prayers in Arabic five times a day (at sunrise, midday, mid-afternoon, sunset, and an hour after sunset). While it is best to do so in a mosque, it is not necessary; likewise, worshippers should face toward Mecca.

3. **Charity** *(Zakah)*: Every Muslim is expected to give to charity what he or she has left after his or her basic needs have been met.

4. **Fasting** *(Sawm)*: During the month of Ramadan, Muslims must not eat, drink, smoke, or have sexual relations between sunrise and sunset. In addition, they are told to avoid anger, greed, lust, and other vices. Muslims believe that they make these sacrifices to learn self-control and to remember the less fortunate. Sharing in the fast also strengthens the bonds of community among Muslims around the world.

5. **Pilgrimage** *(Hajj)*: At least once in their lifetime, Muslims who are able to are expected to make a pilgrimage to the holy city of Mecca in Saudi Arabia. Many traditions

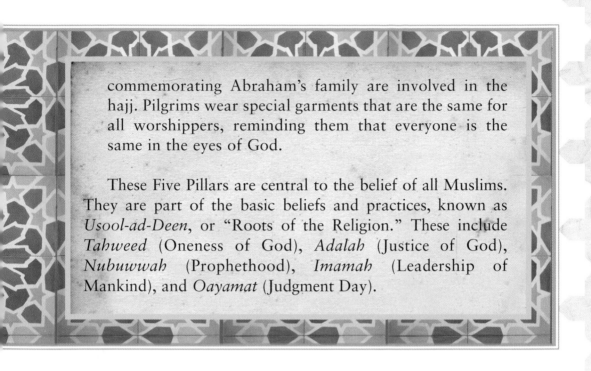

commemorating Abraham's family are involved in the hajj. Pilgrims wear special garments that are the same for all worshippers, reminding them that everyone is the same in the eyes of God.

These Five Pillars are central to the belief of all Muslims. They are part of the basic beliefs and practices, known as *Usool-ad-Deen*, or "Roots of the Religion." These include *Tahweed* (Oneness of God), *Adalah* (Justice of God), *Nubuwwah* (Prophethood), *Imamah* (Leadership of Mankind), and *Oayamat* (Judgment Day).

Arabia's trade routes, but on the fees paid by pilgrims to the Kaaba. Muhammad's message that the gods whose idols were housed at the Kaaba were false threatened the rulers' profits and their control of Mecca. These rulers began a long period of persecuting the new converts of Islam, the followers of which are called Muslims. "Islam" means "submission," specifically, to the will of God (Allah in Arabic). Some Muslims immediately fled Mecca to Abyssinia (present-day Ethiopia), although many remained in Arabia with Muhammad.

In 622, with his own clan no longer protecting him, Muhammad and his followers left Mecca and traveled to

Medina (also known as Madinah). Welcomed into the city, Muhammad helped end the strife between its rival clans, and many converted to Islam. This journey, called the Hijra, marks the beginning of the Islamic calendar.

War soon began between the cities. Muhammad took advantage of a temporary truce in 628 to make a pilgrimage to Mecca, but hostilities soon broke out again. In 630 Muhammad returned at the head of a large army and the people of Mecca surrendered without a fight. Muhammad destroyed the idols in the Kaaba and made Mecca the spiritual center of the Muslim world. (Even today, devout Muslims continue the tradition of praying in the direction of Mecca five times a day no matter where they are on the globe.) Two years later, in 632, Muhammad died, having established a new faith that would soon spread throughout the Mediterranean world.

After the conquest of Mecca, Muslims were the dominant force in Arabia. In the remaining two years of Muhammad's life, the followers of Islam unified the region for the first time. Soon, Muslims began to spread Islam beyond its boundaries, sweeping into Syria and Mesopotamia. Inspired by Islam's message, exceptionally skilled in desert fighting, and mounted on the finest horses in the world, Muslim armies proved unstoppable. The exhaustion of the Byzantine and Persian empires after their long wars created a void that Muslim rushed to fill.

By 660, nearly thirty years after the death of Muhammad, Muslim armies had conquered Egypt and Persia. Over the next five to seven centuries, many Christians, Jews, and Zoroastrians converted to Islam. The two most ancient empires in the Mediterranean had fallen almost without a fight to the Muslim armies, leaving them in control of the ancient Mesopotamian region. Within 100 years of Muhammad's death, Muslims had conquered all of North Africa. In the east they stood at the frontiers of India; and in the west, they prepared to invade Europe.

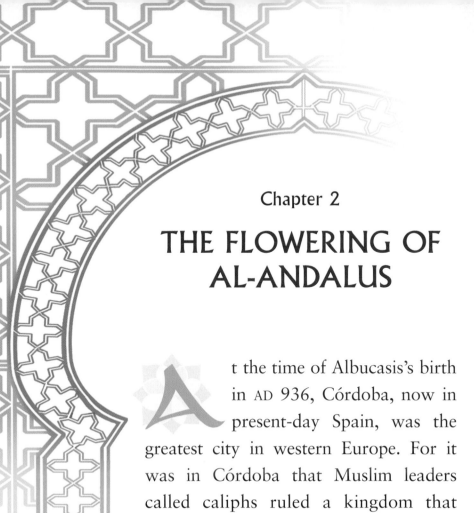

Chapter 2

THE FLOWERING OF AL-ANDALUS

t the time of Albucasis's birth in AD 936, Córdoba, now in present-day Spain, was the greatest city in western Europe. For it was in Córdoba that Muslim leaders called caliphs ruled a kingdom that rivaled any in Europe or the Middle East. The caliphs presided over courts of scholars whose names would later become famous not only in the Muslim world but

The Great Mosque of Córdoba, its bell tower (formerly a Muslim minaret), and a Roman bridge can be seen in this contemporary photograph. In AD 936, when Albucasis was born, al-Andalus (Andalusia) was the name for Muslim territory on the Iberian Peninsula. Islam was its predominant faith. Although the majority of al-Andalus's citizenry converted to Islam, there also existed a population of Jews and Christians in the region who lived peacefully among the Muslims.

all across Christian Europe. Long after the Europeans had discovered their own Greek heritage, these caliphs would be honored for their work in preserving and expanding the wisdom of the ancient Greek and Roman world.

But how did Córdoba become an Muslim capital to rival the city that had once ruled the world? And how was it that Arabic, not Latin, was the language of its scholars? How had a sleepy Spanish town come to rival Baghdad, where the successors to the Prophet ruled over an empire that rivaled the Roman world at its height? To understand the rise of Córdoba, one needs to first examine the history of Spain and its place in the Mediterranean world.

A SHORT HISTORY OF SPAIN

Prior to the emergence of Islam in Arabia, various groups had moved into the Iberian Peninsula, the large boxy region of Europe that today includes Portugal and Spain. These groups included the Celts, who dominated northern Europe until the rise of the Romans. By the ninth century BC, three major groups dominated the Iberian region: the Celtic tribesmen in the interior, Greek colonies on the eastern Mediterranean coast, and the colonies of Phoenicians (a people originally from the region of present-day Lebanon who had created a large trading empire in North Africa) on the southern coast.

The Phoenician domination of the Mediterranean, specifically in the North African city of Carthage, brought it into conflict with the Roman Empire. Eventually the Romans and Phoenicians fought a series of conflicts known as the Punic Wars (from the Latin word for "Phoenician") from 264 BC to 146 BC. Spain played a key role in the second Punic War. The great Carthaginian general Hannibal (247–181 BC) led an army of 40,000 men and several elephants over the Pyrenees and the Alps and into Italy itself. There he defeated several Roman armies before eventually retreating to Carthage to defend it from a Roman invasion. Despite Hannibal's efforts, Carthage lost the second war and with it its Spanish colonies. Rome would triumph in the third war, destroying the city of Carthage and assuming full mastery of the Mediterranean world.

For another two centuries the Romans struggled to complete their conquest of the Iberian Peninsula. They battled the Celts, Greeks, and remaining Phoenicians until it was finally unified under their control during the reign of Augustus (63 BC–AD 14), the first Roman emperor, beginning in 27 BC. Spain quickly became one of the empire's most important provinces. Its olive trees, first brought by the Greeks, were an important export then as they are now. Eventually, the people of Spain were granted full Roman citizenship, an indication of how important the province was to the empire. The Roman emperor Trajan (AD 53–117) (whose magnificent

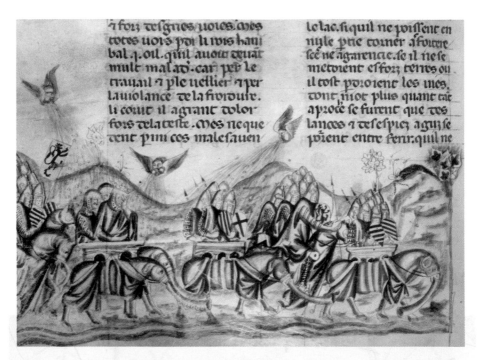

The second Punic War (218–202 BC) is the subject of this manuscript illustration that shows the Carthaginian general Hannibal crossing the Alps with his war elephants and army. This conflict between the Romans and the Phoenicians began during the first Punic War (264–241 BC) under Hannibal's father, Hamilcar Barca. Its purpose was to suppress Roman dominance in the Mediterranean and gain control over resources in the Iberian Peninsula. Three wars were fought over more than a century with the Romans emerging victorious.

column commemorating his victory over the Dacians still stands in Rome) was also born in Spain.

The Romans contributed greatly to Spain and Spanish culture. They built roads and aqueducts that still stand today. They offered the Latin language, the ancestor of modern Spanish. But perhaps the most important thing they brought to Spain, which would have a tremendous impact on its future history, was Christianity. First appearing in

Spain in the first century AD, Christianity by the end of the Roman period was firmly established as the leading religion of Spain. In fact, in many regions of Spain it was the bishops of the early Christian church who preserved order when the Romans could no longer do so.

As the empire collapsed, the barbarians who had attacked it moved deeper into Roman territory and began to rule the former provinces as independent kingdoms. In many cases, the word "barbarian" is inaccurate. Many of the people from outside the borders of the empire had tried to acquire Roman culture and ways; they spoke Latin (or at least the educated among them did), and tried to emulate the grandeur of the Roman rulers. But in many ways they were very different. Instead of the regimented hierarchies of the Roman army and government, strong military leaders governed German tribes. Tribal and family loyalty was more important than an abstract concept of "national" unity. The Europe the barbarians ruled was very different from the stable ideal of *Pax Romana*, a Latin term meaning "Roman peace" that the earlier Roman government had brought to the regions its leaders had conquered.

THE FALL OF THE ROMAN EMPIRE

The fifth century was a chaotic, unstable time for western Europe. The old Roman imperial system was swept away by the barbarian invasions, but the barbarians fought each other as well as the Romans; warfare was nearly constant in some regions. Without the Roman army, banditry reappeared, and whole regions of Italy were devastated. Desperate for protection, the people of villages and towns turned to warlords and their armed bands to protect them. In many cases, barbarians provided this protection in exchange for support of the leader and his men. Before long, the system of feudalism arose from these basic relationships that dominated European government for the next 1,000 years.

Around the 460s, Spain was fully conquered by a Germanic people known as the Visigoths, a name meaning "West Goths." Capturing the region more or less intact (with only a small part of the peninsula held by the Byzantine Empire), they at first ruled Spain from the city of Toulouse (in present-day France) until they were driven out of the region by another Germanic tribe, the Franks. Establishing a new capital at the city of Toledo, the Visigoths consolidated their power until they ruled the largest unified kingdom in western Europe.

The Visigoths ruled Spain as outsiders. They were forced to rely upon their military strength in order to maintain order. Two factors kept their leadership relatively weak, however. First, the Visigoths elected their king from the highest-ranking nobles that led to frequent struggles for

This page is from the *Breviary of Alaric*, a Visigothic code of law issued in 506 by King Alaric II, the Visigothic king of Spain between 484 and 507. The Visigoths lacked a central system of government, and they often relied upon force to keep a hold over their territory in Spain.

the crown. Second, their lack of a governing system left controlling such a large kingdom extremely difficult. (Because of this lack of government, the Visigoths frequently relied upon Christian bishops to help them run the country. This reliance upon the church for control is among the reasons why religion became so crucial to Spain.)

The Visigoths, however, were also responsible for many achievements. As noted earlier, Spain was the largest Christian kingdom in Europe at the time. In the seventh century, a single legal code, which combined elements of Roman law and German traditions, was put into place throughout the kingdom. This was a major advance that was centuries ahead of how the rest of Europe was governed. During this period, Spain remained a rich region vital to Mediterranean commerce, a fact that later contributed to its downfall.

Across the Strait of Gibraltar, in the regions of Africa we today call Morocco, Algeria, Tunisia, and Libya, there lived a nomadic people called the Berbers who inhabited mountainous and harsh desert terrain. They are and were a tough people, well adapted to living in the desert and preserving their nomadic heritage. They had fought against the Romans, who had called the region Mauritania or "the Land of the Moors," which is what the Spanish called them.

As Muslim armies spread into North Africa they came in contact with these peoples and made alliances with them. The Berbers converted to Islam, extending the rule of the caliphs, as

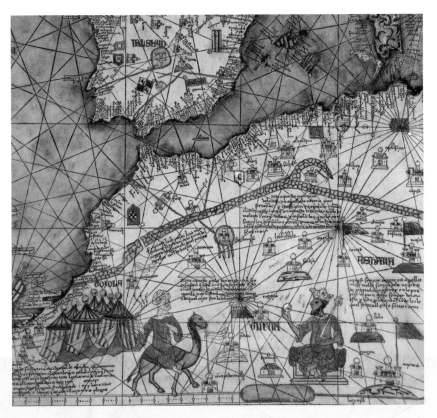

Spain and North Africa are featured on this detail of the *Catalan Atlas*, often noted by historians and scholars to be among the most accurate maps of the fourteenth century. Cresques Abraham (1325–1387), a member of the Majorcan cartographic school, produced the map in 1375. Besides using all known geographical information from the period, cartographers also added information on the map that was drawn from the popular narratives of thirteenth- and fourteenth-century travelers such as Marco Polo.

the successors of Muhammad were called. Soon the Arabs and Berbers (together known as Moors) were raiding the southern coast of Spain, forming an intimate connection that the two regions would share for the next 700 years.

In AD 710, a dispute broke out between the family of the previous king and Rodrigo (Roderic) (?–711), a powerful Visigothic duke who had seized the throne for himself. Rodrigo's opponents appealed to Musa ibn Nusair (640–715), the governor of the Muslims in North Africa. He sent his best general, Tariq ibn Ziyad (?–720), with a small

This fifteenth-century manuscript illustrates Duke Rodrigo (Roderic), the self-appointed Christian Visigothic leader who became king after the death of King Witiza in 710. During the period of Visigothic leadership in Spain, the region suffered great instability. Because of civil war and simultaneous invasions by barbarians from the north and the Moors from the south, Rodrigo was unable to maintain control over the Iberian Peninsula. While attempting to fend off barbarians, he and his army were ambushed in southern Spain by Moors. Greatly outnumbered, Rodrigo was killed in 711, and Spain fell under Muslim control in 718. Christian legends note that Rodrigo was responsible for the Muslim takeover of Spain.

army, across the Strait of Gibraltar and into southern Spain. They landed near an enormous mountain of rock, which later was named after Tariq: Jabal Tariq—Tariq's Rock, or as we know it, the Rock of Gibraltar.

If Rodrigo's opponents had hoped that the Muslims were simply interested in war booty and would leave as soon as

Rodrigo and the Prophecy

Many legends exist about the fall of Spain to the Moors. One of the best known concerns the last Visigothic king of Spain, Rodrigo. According to the legend, two old men came to visit the king in the capital city of Toledo one day. They told him that there was an enchanted tower near the city, with a heavy iron gate. On that gate were many locks, for the tower contained a terrible secret that would bring destruction to anyone who knew it. Because of this, each king had added his own lock to the tower, twenty-seven in all, and no one had ever tried to pass through the gate.

Rodrigo, being brash and arrogant, immediately left with his entire court and went to the tower. He made the two old men open all the locks, and then he stepped inside. Beyond the entrance he found a giant statue made of metal that swung a heavy mace all around, striking the ground with all its might. But Rodrigo saw the words "I only do my duty" stamped on the statue's chest, and when he told it that he merely wanted to learn the secret of the tower, it stopped and allowed him to pass. He went up long flights of stairs until he came to a room at the top of the tower.

In this room was a casket studded with gems. Rodrigo opened it and found a single piece of parchment. On it was a painting of two Moors on horseback, with scimitars (curved Arabian swords) and bows, and above them was written "Behold, rash man, those who shall hurl thee from thy throne and subdue thy kingdom."

they had defeated the king, they were mistaken. In 711, at the battle of Guadalete, Tariq's army decisively beat the Visigoths and killed Rodrigo; the entire Visigoth kingdom of Spain was left defenseless. The Moors had not come to share the region; they had come to conquer it.

LAND OF THE MOORS

The conquest of Spain proceeded with the same speed that had characterized the earlier Muslim conquests of Arabia, Persia, and North Africa. By 719, almost the entire Iberian Peninsula was under the control of the Moors. There was only one small section of the far north, along the Atlantic coast, where a Christian state survived. This was the tiny kingdom of Asturias, founded by a survivor of the Battle of Guadalete. The modern Spanish state would one day emerge from this small Christian outpost, but that day was more than 800 years away. The Moors continued to press on into Europe, storming over the Pyrenees to conquer France. Once there, they conquered some of the region around Toulouse; but in 732, the Franks, under the leadership of Charles Martel (688–741, the grandfather of Charlemagne) defeated them at Poitiers. Afterward, the Moors were content to rule the Iberian Peninsula and did not attempt further invasions of France.

At the time of the Muslim conquest, the Muslim world was ruled from Damascus, the ancient city in Syria. During that period, Damascus was home to the Umayyad family, who had assumed the leadership of the Muslim territories after a struggle with the followers of Muhammad's nephew Ali in 661. (This conflict ultimately led to the split between Sunni Muslims and Shia Muslims, who followed Ali and believed that the Prophet had intended him to be his successor.) The Umayyad caliphs appointed governors, or emirs, to rule over Spain (which was considered part of the province of North Africa, including Morocco), but their actual power was weak.

In 750, however, the Umayyads were overthrown by another family, the Abbasids, who moved the capital from Damascus to Baghdad, a city they founded in what is now Iraq. Although most of the Umayyad family was killed by the Abbasids, one Umayyad prince, Abd al-Rahman (750–788), survived. He made his way to Spain, arriving in 756, and quickly established himself as the sole ruler of the region. For the next 300 years descendants of Abd al-Rahman ruled a region of Spain, or al-Andalus. In 929, Abd al-Rahman III (891–961) took the title of caliph for himself, challenging the Abbasids for dominance as leader of all Muslims. Abd al-Rahman was ruler not just of al-Andalus, but of parts of North Africa as well. As a symbol of the splendor of the caliphate, Abd al-Rahman constructed a new city, Medinat al-Zahra, on a hillside near Córdoba to serve as the administrative center of his government. It was here in this magnificent city of olive groves, palm trees, and gardens that Albucasis was born in 936.

CÓRDOBA'S SPLENDOR

The caliphate of Córdoba would become one of the most advanced states in either Europe or the Muslim world. Scientists and philosophers to rival any of those in Baghdad lived and worked in al-Andalus. While the great works of antiquity were quietly forgotten in a Europe riddled with plague and concerned with day-to-day survival, in al-Andalus they survived and were studied and translated into Arabic with great reverence. Every educated man in al-Andalus possessed a library that would have shamed even the rulers of France and Germany.

The caliphate was advanced in other ways as well, especially when it came to the tolerance of religions other than Islam. In Europe heretics were often burned, Jews were discriminated against and forced to live apart from Christians, and Muslims were sometimes the target of attacks. In al-Andalus there was a mutual respect between these religious groups. Jews held high positions in the government of the caliphate, while Christians were allowed to practice their religion more or less unmolested. Indeed, Toledo had a

bishop who served as an important liaison between the caliphate and the Holy Roman Empire.

The greatest symbol of the power of the caliphate was its capital city, Córdoba; and the greatest monument in Córdoba was its mosque, known as La Mezquita. This enormous structure, the largest mosque in Spain, took more than 200 years to construct. After the fall of Córdoba in 1236, the Spanish, whose numerous changes tragically marred the mosque's once beautiful architecture, turned it into a Christian church.

Only in a place of such fabulous learning and achievement could a climate rich enough for true advancement of science arise. Albucasis's skill was so great that at about twenty-five years of age he became the court physician for al-Hakam II (914–976), the ruler of al-Andalus from 961 to 976. Albucasis was soon the greatest Muslim physician, with a fame destined to eclipse that of even the great doctors of the ancient world. But to understand why Albucasis

This interior section of the Great Mosque of Córdoba was designed beginning in 976, during the reign of al-Hakam II. Built on the site where a Roman temple once stood, the construction of the mosque began under the reign of Abd al-Rahman and features the trademark red-and-white striped arch design that decorated many Muslim structures in Spain. The Great Mosque is revered as a stunning achievement of Muslim architecture but is today also considered an interesting integration of Roman, Visigothic, Muslim, and Christian styles.

was so important and revolutionary, we must first examine the body of knowledge that he inherited from the ancient Greeks and Romans. Albucasis himself expressed his admiration and respect of the ancient Greek and Roman physicians when he wrote in *Al-Tasrif*,

> Whatever I know, I owe solely to my assiduous reading of books of the ancients, to my desire to understand them and to appropriate this science; then I have added the observation and experience of my whole life.

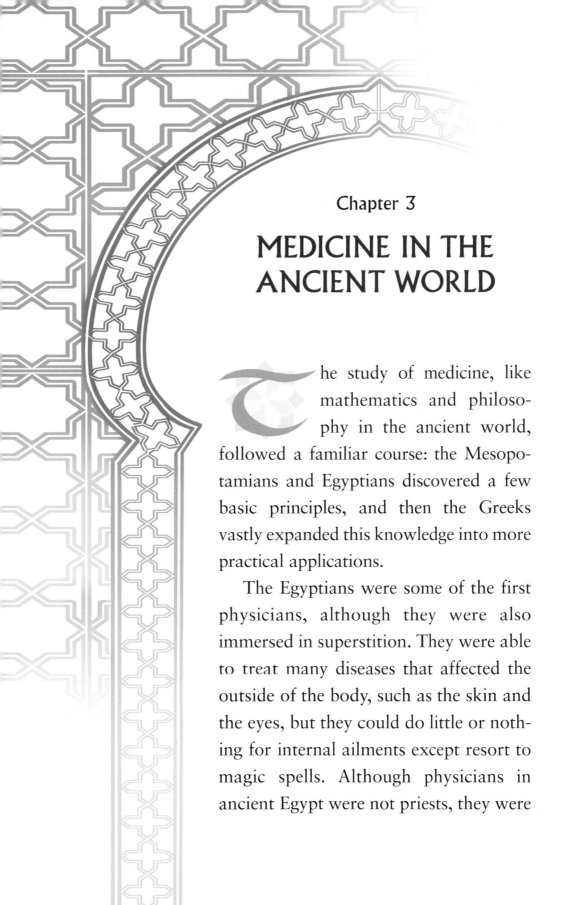

Chapter 3

MEDICINE IN THE ANCIENT WORLD

The study of medicine, like mathematics and philosophy in the ancient world, followed a familiar course: the Mesopotamians and Egyptians discovered a few basic principles, and then the Greeks vastly expanded this knowledge into more practical applications.

The Egyptians were some of the first physicians, although they were also immersed in superstition. They were able to treat many diseases that affected the outside of the body, such as the skin and the eyes, but they could do little or nothing for internal ailments except resort to magic spells. Although physicians in ancient Egypt were not priests, they were

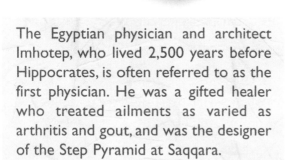

trained at temples where they learned about the use of many drugs, including some still used today. Albucasis later became influential, at least in part, because of his ability to update the findings in the Greek works from *De materia medica*, a source of medicinal plants and drug recipes.

The greatest early Egyptian physician was Imhotep, the architect and mathematician who designed the first pyramid. Oddly enough, although embalming was an advanced art in Egypt (as shown by the many surviving mummies), the Egyptians were not well versed in anatomy. It is for this reason that they attempted only the most basic surgical procedures.

The Mesopotamians also believed in magic, but they showed a surprisingly advanced interest in studying the course and symptoms of diseases. They used a wide variety of medicinal plant derivatives and other remedies, and emphasized the role of rest

The Egyptian physician and architect Imhotep, who lived 2,500 years before Hippocrates, is often referred to as the first physician. He was a gifted healer who treated ailments as varied as arthritis and gout, and was the designer of the Step Pyramid at Saqqara.

and diet in restoring health. The Mesopotamians had a more advanced knowledge of anatomy than the Egyptians had. The Mesopotamian physician was still considered a kind of magician, however, and the study of dreams was an important part of his diagnosis.

HIPPOCRATES

Greek medicine also arose out of superstition. Healing was associated with temples, especially of the gods Apollo and Aesculapius (the god of medicine). Pilgrims would journey to these temples to receive cures, at first from priests, then later from physicians associated with the temple who were called the Sons of Aesculapius or Asclepius. These temple physicians, who were not themselves priests, were the origin of the world's first true physicians.

The unique Greek capacity for synthesizing ideas from other cultures can be seen in the emergence of their medical science. Many of the drugs and treatments that the early Greek physicians utilized had originated in Egypt, whose culture had a distinct influence on the Greeks as demonstrated in their art. However, other ideas were purely Greek in origin and show that profound capacity for logical thought that is the hallmark of this influential people.

From the start, we can observe the Greek use of reason to analyze and diagnose illnesses. Pilgrims who traveled to

Beginning in the ninth century, Arabic translations of important Greek medical texts, such as those by Hippocrates and Galen, became a bridge of knowledge between the ancient and modern worlds. This is the title page to a thirteenth-century copy of *Book of Antidotes (Kitab al-Diryaq)*, which features nine Greek intellectuals, including Pythagoras *(center)*, Andromachus *(bottom right)*, and Galen *(bottom left)*.

the Greek healing centers had to prepare by fasting, cleaning themselves, and praying. Their dreams were interpreted by the priests, but the prescription was usually to change the patient's diet. This emphasis on diet would remain one of the most important characteristics of Greek medicine.

What is important about this process is that each patient's symptoms were studied and compared to other sufferers. In this way, specific diseases began to be identified and treatments for them discovered. This process was aided by the early philosophers, such as Pythagoras (580–500 BC), who took a great interest in the study of medicine.

Eventually, the first medical schools evolved out of the temple schools that instructed the Sons of Aesculapius. The most famous of these was at Cos, an island in the Aegean Sea near the coast of Turkey. This place was famous not only for its shrine to Aesculapius, but because it was home to Hippocrates (circa 460–377 BC), the most influential physician in the history of Europe. Hippocrates was born in Cos, and it was he who first broke the chains of superstition that bound medical study. His basic principles form the basis of all medical research to the present day.

Hippocrates was the first physician to stress the overwhelming importance of observing a patient's symptoms first before deciding what caused them. By diagnosing diseases in this way, they could be described by their symptoms and not their causes (which would have been inaccurate in any case, as the germ theory of disease was 1,500 years in the future). Before Hippocrates, physicians came up with a cause—anything from divine wrath to ingesting the wrong kind of food—and then tried to fit a patient's symptoms into this pattern. Hippocrates reversed this process. Instead of diagnosing a patient's illness by seeing how his or her symptoms fit in with the symptoms of other patients, he identified a patient's symptoms before considering any causes of disease or malady.

Hippocrates also introduced the idea that whatever a patient revealed to a physician should not be revealed to anyone else—a practice enshrined in the famous oath attributed to him. He stressed cleanliness in a physician and insisted that he should always wash his hands before treating anyone. Hippocrates identified many diseases that still plague the world, including pneumonia, typhus, tuberculosis, and arthritis.

Hippocrates strongly believed in the human body's ability to heal itself. He stressed moderation in all things—in eating, drinking, and exercising. Most of his treatments involved treating the symptoms and relieving the suffering of the patient while the disease ran its course—a surprisingly advanced and practical outlook, given that antibiotics lay far in the future.

Hippocrates' real contribution to the art of medicine was that he brought a systematic, logical approach to the study of disease. His followers spread his ideas all through the Greek world, and they followed Alexander into the Middle East. The Romans took up the practice of Hippocratic medicine as well, until it was established throughout the Mediterranean. A large body of writing, the *Corpus Hippocraticum*, attributed to Hippocrates but probably written by his followers, remained part of the medical curriculum well into the nineteenth century.

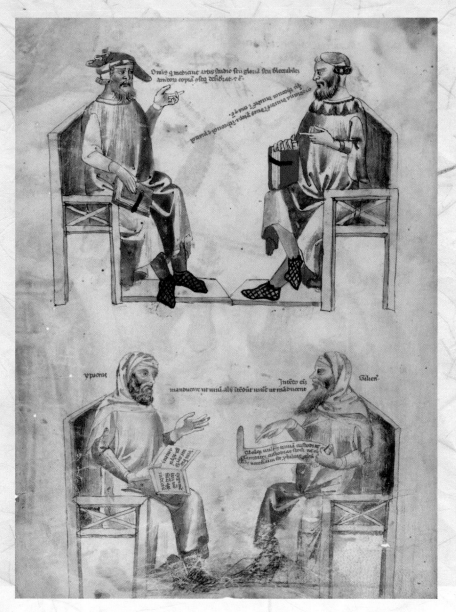

In this fourteenth-century Italian manuscript illustration, ancient Greek physicians Hippocrates *(top and bottom left)* is paired with Galen *(bottom right)*, physician of the ancient Romans, and Hunayn ibn Ishaq, a ninth-century Nestorian Christian from Baghdad who translated more than 130 classical Greek works into Arabic and Syriac. Although the trio did not live simultaneously, this manuscript pays homage to the contribution of Greek physicians to ninth-century Muslim medicine.

The Father of Medicine

The Hippocratic oath is attributed to the brilliant Greek physician Hippocrates, known as the father of medicine. Traditionally, his students swore it when they completed their medical training. Today, doctors continue to take this oath when they graduate from medical school.

Oath of Hippocrates
"Above All, Do No Harm"

I swear by Apollo the physician, and Aesculapius, and Hygeia, and Panacea and all the gods and goddesses, making them my witnesses, that I will fulfill, according to my ability and judgment, this Oath and covenant:

To hold him, who has taught me this art, as equal to my parents, and to live my life in partnership with him, and if he is in need of money to give him a share of mine, and to regard his offspring as equal to my brothers in male lineage, and to teach them this art—if they desire to learn it—without fee and covenant; to give a share of precepts and oral instruction and all the other learning to my sons and to the sons of him who has instructed me, and to pupils who have signed the covenant and who have taken an oath according to the medical law, but to no one else.

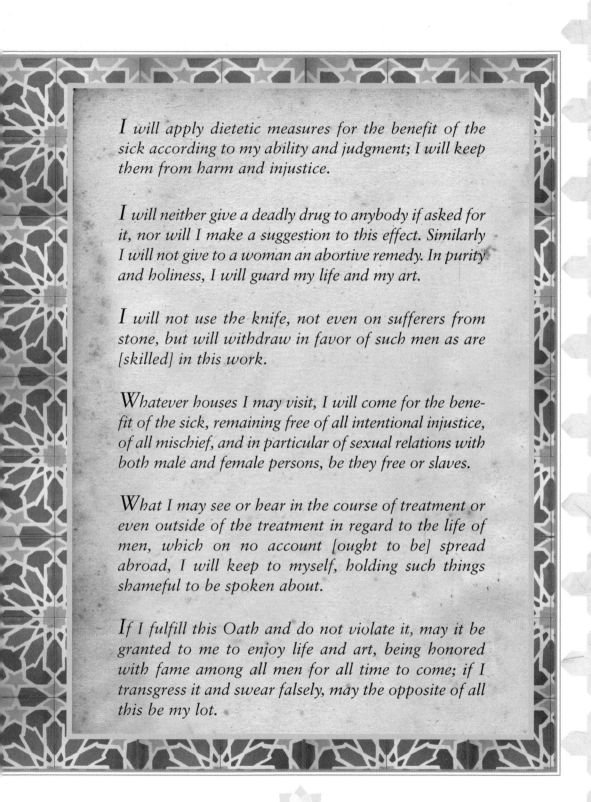

I will apply dietetic measures for the benefit of the sick according to my ability and judgment; I will keep them from harm and injustice.

I will neither give a deadly drug to anybody if asked for it, nor will I make a suggestion to this effect. Similarly I will not give to a woman an abortive remedy. In purity and holiness, I will guard my life and my art.

I will not use the knife, not even on sufferers from stone, but will withdraw in favor of such men as are [skilled] in this work.

Whatever houses I may visit, I will come for the benefit of the sick, remaining free of all intentional injustice, of all mischief, and in particular of sexual relations with both male and female persons, be they free or slaves.

What I may see or hear in the course of treatment or even outside of the treatment in regard to the life of men, which on no account [ought to be] spread abroad, I will keep to myself, holding such things shameful to be spoken about.

If I fulfill this Oath and do not violate it, may it be granted to me to enjoy life and art, being honored with fame among all men for all time to come; if I transgress it and swear falsely, may the opposite of all this be my lot.

This document, known as the Hippocratic oath, dates from 1849. Hippocrates lived sometime between 460 and 377 BC and was known to have written the oath for his students. An updated version of it is still used today in medical schools throughout the world. Great attention was placed on ethics in the Muslim world. Muslim physicians read *Adab al-Tabib* (The Physician's Code of Ethics), which encouraged doctors to speak eloquently, promote modesty and virtue, and avoid excesses.

ARISTOTLE

Other Greeks were also interested in the study of medicine. Many philosophers studied it as part of their attempt to understand the whole of human experience. The greatest of these, Aristotle, although not a physician himself, made important medical contributions through his dissections of animals. He is considered the father of comparative anatomy, since his studies of the anatomy of animals helped the Greeks gain insight into how the human body functions. (His animal anatomy study was specifically useful in the early field of embryology, since he made many observations about the stages of development of chick embryos.) The next great contributor to Greek medicine was Roman citizen Claudius Galen (circa AD 129–199).

GALEN

Galen was born in Pergamum, present-day Bergama, Greece, in a city that had been founded centuries before by Greek immigrants to Asia Minor. Although he preferred to speak Greek for most of his life (perhaps for effect, as Greek was considered a more "learned" language than Latin at the time), he was a Roman citizen and eventually became a physician to four emperors.

As a young man, Galen studied several subjects until settling on medicine, which would turn out to be his true calling. He spent several years traveling to many cities throughout the Greek world to study, including Smyrna, Corinth, and Alexandria, the city in Egypt that had been founded by Alexander the Great and was home to the greatest collection of manuscripts in the ancient world. By

AD 157, he returned to Pergamum, working as a physician for a gladiatorial school. And it was here that Galen acquired valuable knowledge about the nature and treatment of wounds.

Galen's work in Pergamum eventually led him to Rome, where his fame as a physician and writer eventually got him appointed as the court doctor to Emperor Marcus Aurelius (AD 121–180). But it was his work as a writer and experimenter that caused Galen to be the dominant voice in medicine for some 1,200 years.

Galen voraciously devoured the works of Hippocrates and published them with his own annotations. He eventually wrote twenty-two volumes on medical literature, which codified and preserved Hippocratic thinking for centuries. He seized upon the concept of the body's four humors, or fluids (blood, black bile, yellow bile, and phlegm), that at the time was believed to control the body's functioning. Although he used this theory to explain the causes of many diseases, it has since been disproved. Because he believed in the concept of the four humors, and that a disproportionate ratio of humors in the human body often resulted in disease, Galen especially advocated the use of bloodletting, or draining blood from patients, and purging, or inducing vomiting, as treatments.

Galen, however, made many positive contributions to medical science. He dissected both living and dead animals, studying their internal structures in order to learn how similar structures worked in human beings. He was the first physician to prove that the arteries and veins carried blood, not air as had been previously thought. He believed that the brain was the source of thought, not the heart as Aristotle and others had believed. He identified the major nerves of the body and performed some of the earliest tests on them.

Although he was not a Christian, Galen followed the belief of some Greek philosophers that there was a single creator of the world. Because of this, he was accepted by later Christian and Muslim thinkers who might otherwise have dismissed him as a pagan and not worthy of reading. This fact preserved much of his work to the present day.

Although Galen was in many ways a brilliant scientist who was far ahead of his time, in other ways he failed the spirit of his great master, Hippocrates. Although he made many strides in exploring human anatomy, he was also content to assert his ideas as facts without finding any evidence to support them. For example, Galen assumed that a structure called the rete mirabile, a complex network of blood vessels that exists in many hoofed animals, must exist in the neck of humans because he had observed it in sheep. He assigned many important functions to this "organ," although humans do not have this structure.

Although Galen thought that blood was vital to human life—he associated it with the pneuma, or life force—he

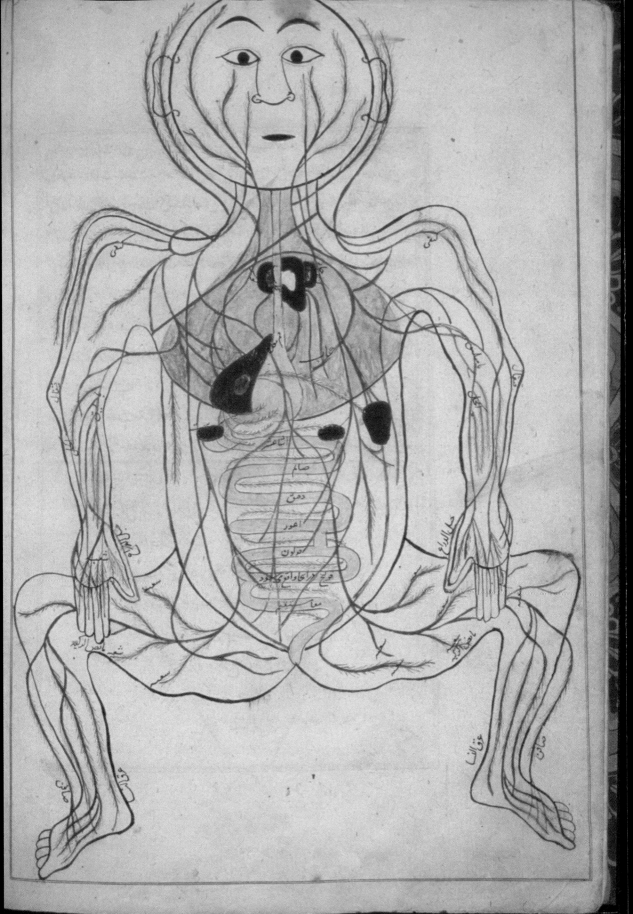

made several errors in describing how it flowed through the human body. Galen believed that blood was not circulated, but merely accumulated in the body (this was also why he endorsed bloodletting to remove the supposed excesses of blood that he felt caused diseases). He thought that the heart sucked blood into it from the veins, and that the arteries were responsible for pumping blood through themselves. He had only a rudimentary understanding of how the lungs passed air into the body, although he did understand that this was the reason that arterial blood was bright red and venous blood was bluish.

Galen's success and brilliance was as an organizer of the Hippocratic method into a system that was superior to any other system of medicine in the ancient world. His techniques lived on and were a profound influence on later Islamic physicians, especially Albucasis. Although Galen failed in capturing and extending the true spirit of Hippocrates, he was willing to examine diseases to try and

This drawing of the body's system of veins is from a Persian manuscript possibly related to the *Tashrih-i Mansuri*, a work of anatomy credited to a fourteenth-century scholar. The diagram was probably included to assist physicians in identifying specific points on the body suitable for bloodletting, which had a 3,000-year history beginning with the Egyptians. Bloodletting was originally believed to remove "evil spirits" from the body, while more "modern" uses were to treat hypertension or internal bleeding. Bloodletting was discontinued during the nineteenth century.

find their causes. Unlike Hippocrates, Galen preferred to reason from a supposed cause to an effect. His system lasted for 1,000 years because of its effectiveness; but at the cost of stifling further research into the real causes of human illnesses.

Galen lived at the height of the Roman Empire. After his death around AD 199, the empire began its long decline toward its ultimate demise in the fifth century. The centuries that followed the fall of the Roman Empire were responsible for the complete stagnation (and in many cases, total loss) of medical and scientific knowledge in Europe. It would be left up to the rising new power of Islam to expand medical knowledge. In the five centuries after the birth of Muhammad, several Muslims would be considered among the greatest physicians in history.

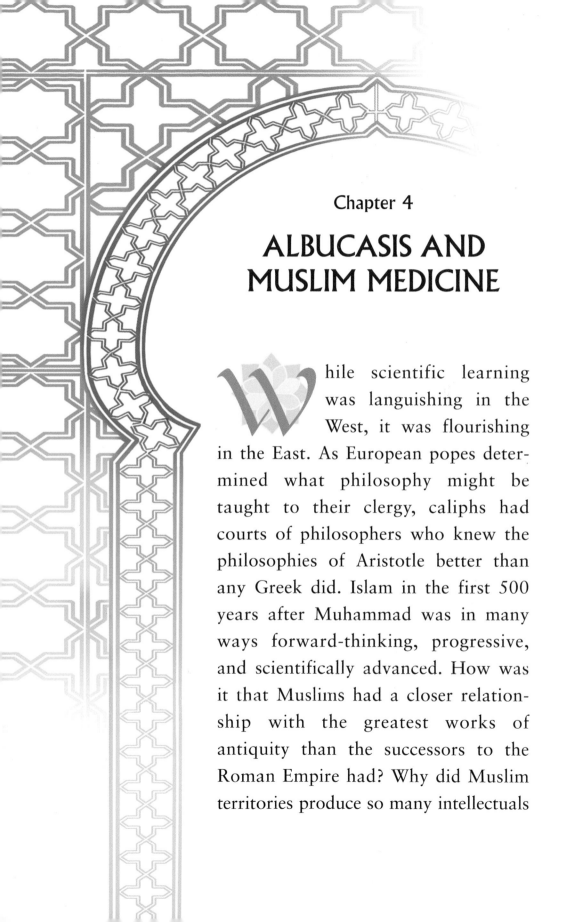

Chapter 4

ALBUCASIS AND MUSLIM MEDICINE

hile scientific learning was languishing in the West, it was flourishing in the East. As European popes determined what philosophy might be taught to their clergy, caliphs had courts of philosophers who knew the philosophies of Aristotle better than any Greek did. Islam in the first 500 years after Muhammad was in many ways forward-thinking, progressive, and scientifically advanced. How was it that Muslims had a closer relationship with the greatest works of antiquity than the successors to the Roman Empire had? Why did Muslim territories produce so many intellectuals

بزان وائی تواند شذ وآنرا سبب شفا شمرد وبازا عمال خیر وسخن توسعه آخرت ازعلت کاه ازان
کونه شفای دهذکه معاودت صنف بنندذ ومن یحکم این مقدمات ازعلم طب نثرا نموفم یق

ونهمت برطلب دین صروف کردانیدم والحق والق راه آنرا دراز و بی بایان یافتیم سراسر مخاوف ومضایق اکله سه

In this fourteenth-century Persian manuscript illustration, a physician takes the pulse of one of his patients during a consultation. Pulse rates were often taken to help diagnose patients. Among one of the most famous physicians said to have used a patient's pulse rate to aid in his diagnosis was the Persian Ibn Sina (Avicenna, AD 980–1037).

and scientists during a period when scientific advancements were declining in Europe? To answer these questions, and to understand how it was that Spain produced the single greatest physician not only of the Middle Ages but since the days of antiquity, we must return to the early days of the Muslim conquests.

When the Muslim armies swept into Syria, they were entering a region of the world that had been thoroughly Hellenized since the time of Alexander the Great. Then a part of the Byzantine Empire, Syria remained a treasure trove of Greek knowledge and learning, although by this time some of it had been deliberately ignored by Christians who considered some of the work of the Greeks to be contrary to Christian doctrine.

Muslims, too, would reject some Greek learning as unsuitable for the faithful. But in other areas, especially medicine, they eagerly devoured the wisdom of the Greek world.

Further expansion into Mesopotamia merely increased Muslim access to Greek works, as these regions had also been part of both Alexander's Macedonian Empire and the Roman and Byzantine empires. Moreover, the Muslim conquests brought Muslims into contact with the ancient cultures of Persia and India.

Although Persia had never regained the preeminence it had enjoyed in the fifth century BC, it remained a civilization of great sophistication and its power was still strong in the region. Contact with Persia was a shock that permanently affected Muslim civilization (and laid the groundwork for some later conflicts, as Persia would ultimately become a Shia region while Arabia and much of the rest of the Muslim world would remain Sunni). Persian art, literature, and poetry permeated and influenced the Muslim territories. Before long, the love of learning and knowledge that the Persian rulers had inspired at their court became the model that the caliphs used to guide their own empire. The ideal Muslim prince was no longer just a fierce mounted warrior; after contact with the Persians, he was also expected to be a poet and scholar.

On the frontiers of Persia, the Muslim armies entered India, eventually subduing most of the northwest region of the subcontinent, the area of present-day Pakistan, and exposing its people to Islam. The people of India also made important contributions to Islamic science and medicine, especially in the study of various medicinal herbs and drugs. The medical traditions founded by the Arab conquerors of northern India are still practiced there to this day.

These changes to the Muslim territories produced an age of great philosophers, men who advanced human knowledge not only about the treatment of diseases, but in mathematics, physics, and chemistry. In medicine, this would culminate in the work of Albucasis, but he built upon a

This fresco dates from the Umayyad dynasty, around AD 730. It reveals some of the decorative influences on the Muslim world as Islam expanded into Mesopotamia and came in contact with both Persian and Indian art. Advancements into these regions also increased the reach of Muslim philosophy.

foundation of many other important thinkers, including the greatest philosopher of al-Andalus.

RHAZES

The Persian philosopher and physician Abu Bakr Muhammad ibn Zakariya al-Razi, known in the West by his Latin name, Rhazes (or Rasis), lived from about 865 to 925. Like Galen, he had pursued many professions before

becoming a physician, including being a jeweler, money-changer, lute player, and alchemist. Problems with his vision led him to seek medical treatment and then apply his formidable mind to the practice of medicine.

Rhazes was widely read in the works of the Greek philosophers and physicians, and he incorporated much of their

The Persian philosopher and physician Abu Bakr Muhammad ibn Zakariya al-Razi, or Rhazes, is pictured in his laboratory in Baghdad in this undated engraving. Rhazes is often considered among the top physicians of the tenth century. In Baghdad, Rhazes was placed in charge of the Muqtadari Hospital, where he sometimes acted as a chemist to mix drugs for patients. He was also a prolific writer and became the first physician to use opium as an anesthetic.

thinking into his own. More important, he followed their example of examining evidence empirically (by experimentation or observation) and using reason to understand the actual causes of events. Rhazes was a great experimenter and a careful observer of physical and biological phenomena. A prolific writer, he wrote more than 100 books on alchemy, philosophy, and medicine. One of these is *Doubts About Galen* (*Shukuk 'ala alinusor*), in which he finds fault with the great Greek physician in many areas, including the theory of the humors. More important, he correctly realized that in many places Galen had presented theories as facts without any evidence to support them. Rhazes also made several other important contributions to medical knowledge, including identifying measles and smallpox as separate diseases, the identification of asthma as a disease, and a study of seasonal allergies. He was the first to realize that fever was a defense mechanism of the body and a natural part of its fight against disease. He also was an accomplished chemist and pharmacist. Not only did Rhazes gather lists of known drugs and publish them in one manuscript, he also introduced many treatments of his own. He was the first to use opium as an anesthetic, he discovered sulfuric acid, and he perfected or created many of the tools, such as the mortar and pestle, of the pharmacists trade. In his belief that a physician must also be a philosopher—today we would say scientist—there was a revival of the true spirit of Hippocratic inquiry that had been lost after Galen.

AVICENNA

Another important Muslim physician and philosopher—and one who had a direct influence on Albucasis—was Ali al-Husain ibn Abdallah ibn Sina, known in the

Ali al-Husain ibn Abdallah ibn Sina, or Avicenna, is shown in this contemporary portrait. Like Rhazes, Avicenna was an influential Persian scholar, physician, and writer. Known as the prince of physicians, Avicenna's masterpiece, *Kitab al-Qanun fi Al-Tibb* (Canon of Medicine) was used as a text in European medical schools for at least 500 years after his death. The *Canon* covered an extensive amount of information on topics such as anatomy, hygiene, fevers, tumors, and fractures.

Arabic-speaking world as Ibn Sina and in the West by his Latin name, Avicenna. He was a child prodigy who had memorized the Qur'an by the age of ten and was a practicing physician by the age of eighteen. As a physician, he made many important advances, developing his own treatments for illnesses. But his true interests lay in philosophy. He read the *Metaphysics* of Aristotle so many times that he memorized it. His works on logic and philosophy are almost unmatched by any other Muslim scholar.

In the West, however, Avicenna is best remembered for his work in medicine, which was comparable to, and in some ways surpassed, the work of Rhazes. He recognized that tuberculosis was an infectious disease, a realization that Europe would not accept until the nineteenth century. His massive book, the fourteen-volume *Canon of Medicine*, (*Kitab al-Qanun fi Al-Tibb*) was a standard reference text in Europe and the Middle East until well into the seventeenth century. His other writings also achieved some prominence in the West, especially his commentaries on Aristotle.

All of these works were certainly known to the man we know as Albucasis. Albucasis was from Medinat al-Zahra, the beautiful administrative city built by the first caliph of Córdoba, Abd al-Rahman. We know relatively little about Albucasis's life because of the destruction of Medinat al-Zahra in 1010, though it was remarkable due to the many advances he made in surgical medicine.

We do know that Albucasis served as the royal physician to the court of one of the later caliphs, al-Hakam II (914–976), and had many students. He was probably of Spanish, not Arabian, descent—one of the Spanish converts

Averroes

The great Muslim physician and philosopher Abu al-Walid Muhammad ibn Ahmad ibn Rushd, known as Ibn Rushd to the Muslim world and Averroes to the West, was one of the greatest geniuses produced by al-Andalus. His works gained him great esteem in Europe, where he was considered one of the most important philosophers of the Middle Ages.

Born in 1126 near Córdoba, he was the son and grandson of important Muslim judges. As a young man he studied philosophy, medicine, and Islamic law. Eventually he would become both a judge and a physician.

In the West, Averroes is best known for his commentaries on Aristotle. Legend has it that one night he had a long conversation with Abu Yaqub Yusuf, the ruler of Córdoba. Averroes so impressed Yusuf with his knowledge of Greek philosophy that the emir asked Averroes to write about Aristotle. Averroes spent the rest of his life on this project, which preserved a treasure trove of ancient Greek writings that might otherwise have been lost forever.

Although he is chiefly remembered as a philosopher and judge, like so many of the great minds of the Muslim world Averroes also worked as a physician, having been appointed to be the personal physician to Abu Yaqub Yusuf. He wrote a major work on the subject, *Al-Kulliyyat* (roughly, *Generalities*). He leaned heavily on the works of Galen, but also added his own unique philosophical perspective.

Averroes is another outstanding example of the influence that the great minds of al-Andalus had on the development of Medieval thought in western Europe, and also of how closely related the disciplines of philosophy and medicine were in the Islamic world.

to Islam who made up an important middle tier of Islamic society in al-Andalus. Albucasis practiced all kinds of medicine, and developed many new techniques. His life's work was a comprehensive encyclopedia of medicine, perhaps the greatest work of its kind written during the Middle Ages, *Al-Tasrif Liman Azija an al-Ta'lif* (usually called *The Method of Medicine*, although the literal translation is, "An Aid to Him that Lacks the Capacity to Read Big Books," probably a reference to the lengthy writings of Avicenna). Although only the last volume, which was dedicated to surgery, became widely known in the West, the work as a whole is truly remarkable and details techniques that would be unknown or uncommon in the rest of Europe for centuries.

What all commentators agree on is that the variety of medical techniques and methods that Albucasis wrote about are truly amazing. Indeed, had he been a Christian of the fifteenth century instead of a Muslim of the tenth, he would be remembered today as a true Renaissance man. The book seems to have been written as a practical guide to his students, whom he refers to as "my children" and about whose welfare he expressed concern.

Like Avicenna, Albucasis believed that the doctor had to closely observe his patient. Reviving the spirit of Hippocratic medicine, he urged doctors to behave ethically toward their patients and he denounced quacks or physicians who offered treatments of doubtful use in return for money.

Perhaps the most valuable thing about *Al-Tasrif* is that it is a record of more than fifty years of the treatments provided by a gifted physician. The case histories, and the way that Albucasis interpreted these cases to make his diagnoses, show that the rational inquiry into the causes and treatment of diseases begun by Hippocrates still survived in Muslim medicine. In fact, *Al-Tasrif* was in many ways an invaluable text for centuries because its wisdom was drawn from Albucasis's direct observations.

Almost every possible medical condition is touched upon in *Al-Tasrif*. But Albucasis was not content to merely record the details he observed in humans. Like Aristotle and Galen, he also dissected animals to compare their internal structures with humans. As an accomplished surgeon, his understanding of the human body far surpassed both Aristotle's and Galen's.

Albucasis made important contributions to nearly every field of medicine. He was very concerned about the successful delivery of babies, or what is now referred to as the field of obstetrics. He was the first person to describe Walcher's position, one in which the woman arches her back and has her knees on the edge of the table; this sometimes helps to make delivery easier. Albucasis was known for training midwives to ensure that they would deliver healthy babies.

Albucasis was very interested in the care of the joints and bones, or orthopedics. In addition to his writings on the surgery of these areas, he described what we know today as

Among Albucasis's greatest achievements was his ability to outline detailed surgical procedures for a variety of ailments. In this fourteenth-century Latin translation of his great work *Al-Tasrif*, several surgical procedures are identified, along with illustrations. Albucasis invented more than 200 surgical instruments, some of which are on display in museums in Córdoba, Spain.

Kocher's technique. This method is used for repairing a dislocated shoulder by careful application of leverage to the dislocated arm while the patient is lying on his or her side. (The West would not discover this technique until the late nineteenth century.) He described the technique of patellectomy, or the removal of the knee bone in cases when it has been smashed. This would not be introduced to the West until 1937. Albucasis also wrote about methods to set bones in simple and compound fractures.

Nearly alone among the physicians of the ancient and medieval world, Albucasis was very interested in dentistry. He described many different dental problems such as misaligned teeth, and suggested ways to correct the flaws. He demonstrated techniques to reimplant teeth that had been knocked out of the mouth. He also described how to make artificial dentures out of the bones of animals.

Albucasis was also among the first surgeons in Europe to practice plastic surgery. *Al-Tasrif* describes several methods of plastic and reconstructive surgery that are still practiced today. He used ink to mark where to make incisions on the faces of his patients. He also described methods of performing breast reduction surgery on women in procedures that greatly resemble contemporary techniques.

Albucasis made his chief contributions to medicine in the field of surgery. The entire last volume of *Al-Tasrif* is dedicated to the subject, and it is the most detailed work of its kind to have been written in the Muslim world. In its meticulous description, accuracy, and inventiveness, *Al-Tasrif* far outstrips any previous work and demonstrates a level of technique unknown prior to Albucasis, even among the Greek masters.

Albucasis was also a practical surgeon. As noted previously, he was interested in repairing damaged joints. He also perfected techniques to remove arrows and heal other wounds.

The urinary system was often of particular interest to Muslim physicians who would examine a patient's urine as a way to diagnose his or her illness. Albucasis carried this examination to a much higher level. He perfected surgical techniques for bladder, kidney, and gallstones. Among the many surgical instruments he invented was a device to examine the urethra, the passage through which urine is expelled, a version of which is still in use today.

Albucasis was the first surgeon to operate successfully on the bowels. He also developed the innovative use of silk and catgut (tough thread made from the intestines of sheep) to stitch wounds shut.

The nervous system was also a curious part of the body to Albucasis, who described many different conditions caused by head and spinal injuries. He developed special tools for drilling into the skull without damaging the brain. He instructed other surgeons to pay particular attention to the anatomy of the skull in order to understand the proper

Albucasis *(left)* is pictured in this sixteenth-century woodcut holding a flask of his own urine, presumably for analysis. Many of Albucasis's treatments and techniques became forerunners of modern medicine. Extracting urine for analysis, for example, did not become commonplace outside of the Muslim world until around 1300.

surgical technique to avoid nerve damage. He demonstrated techniques to heal spinal fractures.

Albucasis was interested, too, in what today we call otolaryngology, or treatment of the ears, nose, and throat. He knew how to set and heal fractures of the nasal bones. He also performed delicate surgeries on the ear, and developed

نوع من النجر آلة مشاكلة لزائدة النجر وافلم أن الاعمال كلها
فربّما تولّدعلى نوع الآلة التي تحتاج إليها إذا دانت معه دربة طويلة
ومعرفة بقانون هذا المنّاعة اذ من مصر المناعة وشاهدنا ضروبا
من مرار وفزربيستنبط لنفسه ما بمشاكلة من الآلات لكل مزيج وأن
مصور لك جميع آخر هذا الأبواب من آلات تفعلها آلة تغني عليهم
وفيما شئنا تغنى بما على عينها ان شاء الله تعالى

صورة منشار

صورة منشار آخر

صورة منشار صغير

صورة منشار آخر كبير

tools to examine and operate on the tiny components of the ear. He detailed how to do tracheotomies and even worked on the eyes, extracting cataracts.

Albucasis showed an unusual concern for the illnesses of women. He was the first physician to describe surgery to treat breast cancer. As mentioned before, Albucasis was an accomplished obstetrician, but he also practiced gynecology. He was able to do surgery to treat gallstones, and he made a special note in *Al-Tasrif* on how to respect the modesty of women when treating them for this condition. One of his most important contributions to the art of medicine was the first use of a mirror to reflect light on a patient during an operation. He developed this technique to examine the cervices of his female patients.

In addition to his many surgical techniques, Albucasis developed a variety of surgical instruments, some of which remain in use today. He may have even invented the humble tongue depressor. Albucasis is also named as the creator of tooth extractors, obstetric devices (including forceps), a

Albucasis invented the surgical instruments on this manuscript page in the tenth century. Many of them remain similar to surgical instruments still in use today. Today's historians and scholars consider Muslim surgical achievements remarkable. While surgery was basically unheard of in Europe during the same period, Muslim physicians such as Albucasis were treating serious wounds, using cauterization techniques, setting broken bones, and even treating cancerous tumors.

hook to remove nasal polyps, syringes to perform enemas, and various surgical knives and saws.

Albucasis was the first physician to identify hemophilia as a hereditary disease; he also perfected the use of cauterization to seal blood vessels, as well as the technique of ligation, or tying off major blood vessels to prevent bleeding.

More than just a technical manual, however, *Al-Tasrif* is a comprehensive set of recommendations for the practice of medicine. It was the first work in the Muslim world to treat surgery as a field of separate study distinct from the normal practice of medicine. Albucasis was very careful in his advice to those who wanted to become surgeons. He demanded that they take time to learn about the entire field of medicine before they attempted to specialize in one specific area, and that they complete their studies of general medicine before they tried to perform surgery. This plan of learning is remarkably similar to our own modern system for training doctors, which requires that all physicians learn the basics of many disciplines before attempting to become specialists.

Al-Tasrif had distinguished Albucasis in yet another important way—in the instruction of future physicians in the preparation of drugs. In the section on pharmacology, *Al-Tasrif* describes many important drug recipes, including ones for laxatives and cardiac drugs.

Just as Galen had codified the learning of antiquity and became the sole authority to which all physicians turned, so, too, did Albucasis codify all that had been learned since by Muslim physicians. His work was a great improvement on Galen's in many ways, for it included far more practical knowledge of human anatomy and was considered among the greatest works on surgery ever written. In time it would displace Galen's work as the most influential medical text in Europe.

Galen and Albucasis were similar in another way as well: both lived during the height of their particular empire. However, the fall of Galen's Rome was several centuries away at the time of his death (and indeed, his part of the world would be ruled by its successor, the Byzantine Empire, for another 1,000 years). Albucasis was not so fortunate. Within his lifetime he saw the collapse of the caliphate, the weakening of Muslim power, and the beginning of the end of the golden age of al-Andalus. It was in this chaotic climate that Albucasis died of natural causes in 1013.

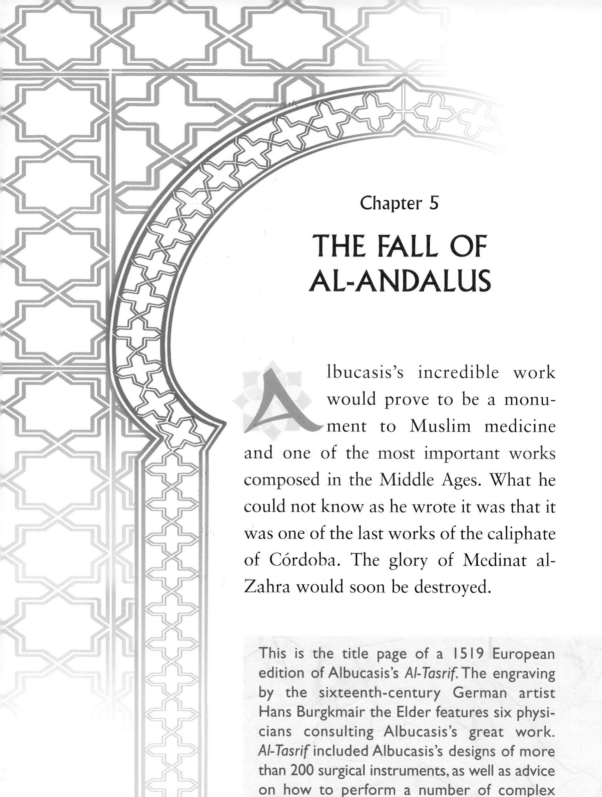

Chapter 5

THE FALL OF AL-ANDALUS

Albucasis's incredible work would prove to be a monument to Muslim medicine and one of the most important works composed in the Middle Ages. What he could not know as he wrote it was that it was one of the last works of the caliphate of Córdoba. The glory of Medinat al-Zahra would soon be destroyed.

This is the title page of a 1519 European edition of Albucasis's *Al-Tasrif*. The engraving by the sixteenth-century German artist Hans Burgkmair the Elder features six physicians consulting Albucasis's great work. *Al-Tasrif* included Albucasis's designs of more than 200 surgical instruments, as well as advice on how to perform a number of complex surgical procedures.

LIBER THEORICAE

NECNON PRACTICAE ALSAHARAVII IN PRI-

sco Arabum Medicorum conuentu facile principis: qui vulgo
Açararius dicitur: iam summa diligentia & cura
depromptus in lucem.

𝕮um priuilegio summi 𝔓ontificis
et 𝔍mperatoris 𝕽omani.

Al-Hakam II, the caliph who had employed Albucasis as his personal physician, died in 976. His nominal successor was his son, Hisham II (966–1009), but power was actually in the hands of the ambitious vizier (prime minister) Abu Amir al-Mansur (938–1002), ("the Victorious"; the title was Latinized to Almanzor, the name he is usually known by in the West) because of his brilliant military campaigns against the Christian kingdoms of northern Iberia. While Hisham was kept occupied with the pleasures of his palace, al-Mansur ran the caliphate for him. His victories over the Christians led to huge amounts of plundered wealth pouring into the coffers of Córdoba.

Although al-Mansur had brought untold riches and glory to the caliphate by his death in 1002, he had also exposed its weaknesses. It was possible for ambitious men to rise to great power and effectively control the government, and the wealth of al-Andalus would lure many to attempt to do so.

Al-Mansur was briefly succeeded by his son, Abd al-Malik (?–1008), but when he died prematurely, civil war broke out in the caliphate. A great-grandson of Abd al-Rahman III seized power from Hisham II and proclaimed himself the new caliph, Muhammad II (880–1010). In North Africa, however, the Berber tribes rebelled and proclaimed a different caliph descendant of Abd al-

Rahman: Suleiman (?–1016). Soon, Berber armies invaded Spain and marched on Córdoba, destroying Medinat al-Zahra in 1010. In a stunning reversal, Muhammad II appealed to the Christians for help, and an army from Castile helped him defeat the Berbers in 1010. Muhammad II was assassinated shortly after that, however, and Hisham II returned to his throne.

Suleiman regrouped while his Berber armies terrorized the countryside. He besieged Córdoba until it surrendered in 1013. Although he would "rule" for three more years, for all intents and purposes the caliphate had been destroyed, although different men succeeded the title until 1031. Al-Andalus fractured completely under the strain of the civil war, breaking up into several small "states" commonly called the *taifa* (Arabic for "party" or "faction") kingdoms.

This presented the Christians with an opportunity they could not ignore. From the humble kingdom of Asturias, far to the north, had emerged several rapidly expanding kingdoms: Navarre, Aragon, and Castile, which together were rapidly becoming the most powerful unification in Spain. Under the leadership of the kings Ferdinand the Great (1016–1065), who held the throne from 1035 to 1065, and Alfonso the Brave (1040–1109), who ruled from 1072 to 1109, Castile led the attacks against the Moors called the Reconquest.

Gerard of Cremona

Muslim civilization preserved many of the writings of the ancient Greeks that would have otherwise been lost. However, much of this work was translated into Arabic, and thus was inaccessible to most scholars of Western Europe. One man, Gerard of Cremona, helped start Europe's intellectual revolution by translating these works into Latin, the language of government, religion, and philosophy in Europe.

We know little about his life. He was born around 1114 in Cremona, a city in Lombardy (a region of northern Italy), where he became a scholar of philosophy. Finding that his Italian teachers did not have many ancient writings available to them—especially the great astronomer Ptolemy's *Almagest*—he decided to try and find copies of these works and translate them himself.

By 1144, Gerard was in Toledo, Spain where he learned Arabic and began working on the translations that made him famous.

Gerard's translation of the *Almagest* was the only one available in Europe until the late fifteenth century, when Greek versions were discovered and translated into Latin. He translated Euclid's *Geometry* and many original works by Muslim scholars. He also translated medical works, including Albucasis's *Al-Tasrif* and the *Canon*. (Some scholars attribute these translations to a later Gerard, Gerard of Sabbionetta.)

Gerard of Cremona died in Toledo in 1187, having laid the foundation for much of the intellectual revolutions of the thirteenth and fourteenth centuries in Europe.

In the left-hand corner of this Italian medical manuscript from 1300, two students are seen gesturing toward a teacher believed to be Albucasis. The scholarship that existed between Muslim physicians and students was rich indeed. In addition to single-handedly preserving important Greek and Roman works, Muslims incorporated all they learned from Syriac, Persian, and Indian sources. Gerard of Cremona, the famous Italian translator of scientific manuscripts, translated this work.

The taifa kingdoms were not up to the task of resisting the Christians, and Castile and Aragon expanded southward into al-Andalus. In 1085, Alfonso captured Toledo, the old Visigothic capital of Spain. And in 1144, Gerard of Cremona

(1114–1187) arrived there to translate as many Arabic works as he could, including Albucasis's *Al-Tasrif*.

From Toledo, *Al-Tasrif* spread throughout Christian Europe, its fame slowly growing. The great French surgeon Guy de Chauliac (1300–1368), in his work *Chiurgia Magna* (*Great Surgery*, itself used as a medical text for more than 300 years) quoted Albucasis more than 200 times. In 1471, *Al-Tasrif* was printed in Venice, and quickly became a standard medical text. As late as the sixteenth century, another great French surgeon, Jacques Dalechamps (1513–1588), was quoting *Al-Tasrif*. Albucasis had well earned his title of "the chief of all surgeons," as Italian translator Pietro Argallata (?–1423) called him in the fifteenth century.

However, as the glory of Albucasis's work increased, that of al-Andalus declined. The fall of Toledo was merely one of the disastrous losses it suffered during the eleventh century; in fact, all of the conquests of the Christians would become permanent. As the Spanish kingdoms gained power, they extracted tribute from the weak taifa kingdoms, rich sums of gold that they used to further their military aims both in Spain and in the Mediterranean.

These conquests attracted the attention of the rest of the Muslim states. In the 1050s, a puritanical movement swept Morocco. Called the Almoravids in Spain (from the Arabic word *al-murabit*, which means "a religious ascetic"), they practiced an especially strict form of Islam.

This fourteenth-century French painting features the famous French surgeon Guy de Chauliac. His book *Chirurgia Magna*, written in 1363, outlined the qualities that make a good surgeon. He wrote, "A good surgeon should be acquainted with liberal studies, with medicine and above all with anatomy; he should be courteous; bold in security, pious and merciful, not greedy of gain, but looking for his fee in moderation, according to the extent of his services." European surgeons working in the fourteenth century continued to benefit from the works of Albucasis.

The continuing success of the Christians caused the leaders of the taifa kingdoms, with great reluctance, to invite the Almoravids into Spain to help them fight the Castilians. Their fears were justified. Although the Almoravids halted the

Christian advance, they soon conquered the taifa kingdoms, which they considered hopelessly corrupt. By 1090, the Almavorids had reunified al-Andalus and North Africa under their rule.

The Almoravid caliphate was far stricter than the Umayyad caliphate had been. It rejected the rich lifestyles the caliphs of Córdoba had once enjoyed. It was also far less tolerant of Jews and Christians than the Umayyad caliphs had been.

However, within fifty years of ruling al-Andalus, the Almoravid caliphs were guilty of many of the same vices of which they had accused the Umayyads. Disunity followed: Arabs against Berbers, natives of Spain against the invading Almoravids. Once again the Christians stepped up their attacks. A new Berber dynasty called the Almohads emerged in North Africa and overthrew the Almoravids.

Almohad was a name taken from the Arabic term *al-muwahhidun* ("monotheist" or "unitarian"). Like the Almoravids before them, they were dedicated to the

In this image taken from a twelfth-century manuscript, the Muslim governor of the Almoravid caliphate is holding a war meeting in his fortified castle, the Alcazar, in Seville, Spain. The Almoravid caliphs were interested in reviving a more conservative Muslim society and did not embrace the religious views of Jews and Christians in quite the same ways as did the earlier caliphs of Córdoba.

purification of Islam and the defeat of the enemy. They swept into Spain and defeated the Christians, holding them back for another century.

Almohad rule became gentler in time, and a second great period of art and literature eventually bloomed under its reign. This was about the time that the great philosopher Averroes (1126–1198) was living and writing in Spain.

The Christian kingdoms continued to gain power in Spain, however, and even the Almohads could not stop their advance. In 1212, the emir Muhammad III al-Nasir (?–1213) was defeated by the combined forces of Castile, Aragon, Portugal, and Navarre at the battle of Las Navas de Tolosa. Within a decade, all of Muslim Spain had been reclaimed by the Christians, except for the small state of Granada on the Mediterranean coast—and Granada paid a huge yearly tribute to the Spanish. In 1469, the marriage of Ferdinand II of Aragon (1452–1516) and Isabella of Castile (1451–1504) united the two largest Spanish kingdoms. Together, in 1492, they defeated Granada and ended the existence of the last Moorish state in Spain, just before they sent Christopher Columbus to the New World.

For 700 years, Muslim states had existed on the European continent, in what would become the most powerful kingdom in western Europe during the sixteenth century. When the Moors invaded Spain, they brought with

This seventeenth-century portrait by Spanish artist Pedro de Mena features the Catholic monarchs of Spain, Ferdinand II, king of Aragon, and his wife, Isabella I of Castile. The couple was married in 1469, a union that joined all of Spain (except for the last Moorish stronghold, Granada, which fell in 1492).

them the only living tradition of the ancient Mediterranean world. Their learning and culture far outstripped that of the barbarian princes they conquered, so much so that they abhorred the pale adversaries from over the Pyrenees and had as little to do with them as possible. As for the Europeans,

Among the most famous architectural structures in all of Spain is the Muslim palace Alhambra. Its exquisite design and decorative mix of geometric, calligraphic, arabesque, and Indian-inspired intertwining vegetation is considered a remarkable Muslim achievement. Built by Nasrid rulers between 1338 and 1390 in Granada, the last Moorish stronghold, it consists of three parts: the royal palace, the fortress of Alcazabra *(pictured)*, and the gardens. Behind the palace walls, Nasrid rulers faced the constant threat of invasion from Christian monarchs, increasing economic hardship, and even the spread of the Black Death, or plague.

they mostly felt disdain for the brilliant people to the south and waged an unceasing war to oust them.

For over 700 years in al-Andalus, a culture thrived that incorporated the best of three worlds: the Muslim world, the ancient Greek world, and the new world of Europe that was unfolding. It was an age of great wealth and great sophistication, of respect for the accumulated wisdom of the past and a thirst for even greater knowledge. During this period of knowledge and learning, many Muslims not only preserved the past, but helped light the way for the future. In the field of medicine, perhaps no man did more than Albucasis.

TIMELINE

476

Year typically given by historians to signify the end of the Roman Empire.

570

The prophet Muhammad is born in Mecca (Makkah).

610

Muhammad receives the first revelations.

632

Muhammad dies.

659

Muslims split into Shia and Sunni sects.

660

Muslim armies conquer Egypt and Persia.

698

Muslims conquer North Africa.

711

Battle of Guadalete takes place between Muslims and Visigoths in Spain.

719

Nearly the entire Iberian Peninsula is in control of the Muslims (Moors).

750

The Umayyad dynasty is overthrown by the Abbasid dynasty; the Abbasid capital is moved to Baghdad.

756

Umayyad prince Abd al-Rahman arrives in Spain and establishes himself as ruler.

785

Construction begins on the Great Mosque of Córdoba.

832

The House of Wisdom is founded in Baghdad; classical Greek works are translated into Arabic.

929

Abd al-Rahman III becomes caliph and rules over Muslims in Spain and North Africa.

936

Albucasis (Abu al-Qasim al-Zahrawi) is born in Medinat al-Zahra, the palace city near Córdoba, Spain.

961

Albucasis becomes court physician of al-Hakam II at the age of twenty-five.

1010

Albucasis's hometown of Medinat al-Zahra is invaded and destroyed by Berber armies from North Africa.

(continued on following page)

(continued from previous page)

1013

Albucasis dies.

1050

Puritanical Almoravid armies gain power in North Africa.

1085

Christian armies under Alfonso the Brave capture Toledo, the old Visigothic capital of Spain.

1363

French surgeon Guy de Chauliac consults Albucasis's *Al-Tasrif*.

1469

The marriage of Ferdinand II, king of Aragon, and Isabella I of Castile nearly unites all of Spain.

1471

Albucasis's *Al-Tasrif* is first printed in Italy.

1492

Last Moorish stronghold in Granada falls to the Christians.

GLOSSARY

Allah "God" in Arabic, the language of Muhammad and Muslims.

arable Fit for cultivation; fertile.

Asia Minor The peninsula of Asia that juts out into the Aegean Sea that forms most of modern Turkey.

Balkan Peninsula A mountainous peninsula in southeastern Europe, where Greece, Albania, Serbia, Bulgaria, and parts of Turkey are today located.

Berbers The tribal people of North Africa. They converted to Islam in the seventh century and formed the bulk of the Muslim armies that invaded Spain in 710.

Byzantine Empire The eastern half of the Roman Empire, which survived for 1,000 years after the fall of Rome. It took its name from the original name of its capital city of Constantinople, Byzantium. The Byzantine Empire ended when the Muslim Turks captured Constantinople in 1453.

caliph The title given to the successors to Muhammad as the temporal leaders of all Muslims. The Umayyad rulers of al-Andalus claimed the title in 929, although many Muslims disputed their right to it.

emir The Arabic word for an important noble who ruled a large region; it could mean "governor" but as these rulers were generally independent, it is probably best to translate it as "ruler."

Five Pillars The core beliefs of Islam, consisting of submission to God, prayer, fasting, charity, and a pilgrimage to Mecca.

Hellenization The spread of Greek culture, philosophy, and language.

Hijra The Arabic term for the move from Mecca to Medina by the prophet Muhammad and his followers in 622. The Muslim calendar begins with this date.

Islam The name of the religion founded by Muhammad, known as the Prophet, in 610. The name means "submission (to God)."

Kaaba The large black rectangular building in Mecca, a sacred site for Muslims. Millions of pilgrims visit Mecca every year to pray at this "house of God."

Mecca The city in central Arabia, the birthplace of Muhammad, that is considered the holiest place of Islam. All Muslims are supposed to pray in its direction five times a day.

Moors The Spanish name given Arabs and Berbers of North Africa.

mosque A Muslim house of worship.

Muslim A follower of Islam.

orthodox Adhering to an accepted or traditional faith, especially in religion.

Persian Empire An ancient empire in the Middle East, comprising what is now Iraq and Iran.

Phoenicians An ancient sea-trading people who lived in what is now Syria and Lebanon. They introduced writing to the Greeks, and their descendants, the Carthaginians, ruled much of the Mediterranean and North Africa until the time of the Romans.

Qur'an The holy book of Islam, sometimes spelled "Koran." It was dictated to the prophet Muhammad by the angel Gabriel. Muslims believe it is the word of God.

schism A separation or division of factions, especially in religion.

Shia Muslims who believe Ali and his descendants are the rightful successors of Muhammad. Shia Muslims represent the majority in present-day Iraq and Iran.

Sunni The largest sect of Islam, who believe that those who uphold Muhammad's Sunnah (example) can be legitimate leaders. Most Arab, Asian, and African Muslims are Sunni.

Syriac An ancient Aramaic language spoken in Syria from the third to the thirteenth centuries.

Umayyad Dynasty of caliphs that ruled the Muslim territories until 750. A lone survivor of the dynasty reached Spain, where his successors would rule until 1036.

Visigoths Germanic tribe that invaded the Roman Empire in the fifth century AD, eventually settling in Spain, where it ruled until being conquered by the Moors.

vizier Arabic title meaning prime minister; the most important official at the court of an emir, or caliph.

Zoroastrianism A religion founded in Persia by Zoroaster and set forth in the Avesta, a collection of sacred texts, believed to be handed down from Zoroaster himself. Zoroastrians believe in a universal struggle between the forces of light and darkness.

FOR MORE INFORMATION

Islamic Medical Association of North America
101 W. 22nd Street
Suite 106
Lombard, IL 60148
(630) 932-0000
e-mail: hq@imana.org
Web site: http://www.imana.org

Islamic Society of North America
6555 South 750 East
Plainfield, IN 46168
(317) 839-8157
Web site: http://www.isna.net

National Library of Medicine (Collection of Islamic
  Medical Manuscripts)
8600 Rockville Pike
Bethesda, MD 20894
(301) 402-8878
Web site: http://www.nlm.nih.gov/hmd/arabic/arabichome.
  html

Walters Art Museum
Collection of Islamic Art
600 North Charles Street
Baltimore, MD 21201-5118
(410) 547-9000
Web site: http://www.thewalters.org

Worcester Art Museum
Collection of Islamic Art
55 Salisbury Street
Worcester, MA 01609
(508) 799-4406
Web site: http://www.worcesterart.org/Collection/
  islamic.html

WEB SITES

Due to the changing nature of Internet links, the Rosen
Publishing Group, Inc., has developed an online list of Web
sites related to the subject of this book. This site is updated
regularly. Please use this link to access the list:

http://www.rosenlinks.com/gmps/albu

FOR FURTHER READING

Browne, Edward Granville. *Arabian Medicine*. Westport, CT: Hyperion Press, 1983.

Collins, Roger. *Early Medieval Spain: Unity in Diversity, 400–100*. New York, NY: Palgrave Macmillan, 1995.

Constable, Olivia Remie. *Medieval Iberia: Readings From Christian, Muslim, and Jewish Sources*. Philadelphia, PA: University of Pennsylvania Press, 1993.

Lowney, Chria. *A Vanished World: Medieval Spain's Golden Age of Enlightenment*. New York, NY: Free Press, 2005.

Menocal, María Rosa. *The Ornament of the World: How Muslims, Jews, and Christians Created a Culture of Tolerance in Medieval Spain*. New York, NY: Little, Brown and Company, 2002.

Porter, Ray, ed. *The Cambridge Illustrated History of Medicine*. New York, NY: Cambridge University Press, 2001.

Turner, Howard R. *Science in Medieval Islam*. Austin, TX: University of Texas Press, 1997.

BIBLIOGRAPHY

Fletcher, Richard. *Moorish Spain*. Berkeley, CA: University of California Press, 1993.

Lane-Poole, Stanley. *The Story of the Moors in Spain*. Baltimore, MD: Black Classic Press, 1990.

Menocal, María Rosa. *The Ornament of the World: How Muslims, Jews, and Christians Created a Culture of Tolerance in Medieval Spain*. New York, NY: Little, Brown and Company, 2002.

Nasr, Seyyed Hossein. *Science and Civilization in Islam*. Cambridge, MA: Harvard University Press, 1968.

Porter, Roy. *The Greatest Benefit to Mankind: A Medical History of Humanity*. New York, NY: W. W. Norton & Company, 1997.

Siraisi, Nancy G. *Medieval and Early Renaissance Medicine*. Chicago, IL: University of Chicago Press, 1990.

Watt, W. Montgomery. *The Majesty That Was Islam*. New York, NY: Praeger Publishers, 1974.

INDEX

About the Author

Fred Ramen's love of history and science has led him to write extensively on both subjects for young people and adults. He received a bachelor's degree from Hufstra University in 1994 and a master's degree from New York University in 1998. His most recent book on the Muslim world is *A Historical Atlas of Iran*.

About the Consultant

Munir A. Shaikh, executive director of the Council on Islamic Education (CIE), reviewed this book. The CIE is a non-advocacy, academic research institute that provides consulting services and academic resources related to teaching about world history and world religions. http://www.cie.org.

Photo Credits

Cover, p. 12 Wellcome Library, London; p. 7 Bayerische Staatsbibliotek, Munich, Germany, Clm 10058, f. 154v; pp. 9, 38–39, 80 Bibliothèque Nationale de France; pp. 15, 20 © 2004 Werner Forman/TopFoto/The Image Works; p. 17 © The British Library: Or. 2784 f.96; p. 18 Erich Lessing/Art Resource, NY; p. 23 © The British Library: Or. 343 f.21; pp. 24, 25, 40, 54, 55, 73, 88 background tiles courtesy of Mosaic House, New York; p. 29 © Peter M. Wilson/Corbis; p. 32 © British Library/HIP/Art Resource, NY; p. 35 Snark/Art Resource, NY; p. 37 © Courtesy of Museum of Maritimo (Barcelona, Spain), Ramon Manent/Corbis; p. 44 Mezquita (Great Mosque) Cordoba, Spain/ Bridgeman Art Library; p. 48 Réunion des Musées Nationaux/Art Resource, NY; p. 50 Oesterreichische Nationalbibliothek, Vienna, Austria, Archives Charmet/Bridgeman Art Library; p. 53 Bibliotheque Nationale, Paris, France, Archives Charmet/Bridgeman Art Library; pp. 56, 71, 79 Courtesy National Library of Medicine; p. 60 © The Trustees of the Chester Beatty Library, Dublin/Bridgeman Art Library; p. 64 The Art Archive/National Library Cairo, Egypt/Dagli Orti; p. 67 Scala/Art Resource, NY; pp. 68–69 © Mary Evans Picture Library/The Image Works; pp. 76, 91 Bridgeman-Giraudon/Art Resource, NY; p. 85 Courtesy Royal College of Physicians of Edinburgh, Scotland; p. 89 Yale University, Harvey Cushing/John Hay Whitney Medical Library: Paneth Codex p. 503. Image provided by the Index of Medieval Medical Images, History & Special Collections, Biomedical Library, UCLA; p. 92 Monasterio de El Escorial, El Escorial, Spain, Index/Bridgeman Art Library; p. 95 Bildarchiv Preussischer Kulturbesitz/Art Resource, NY; p. 96 © Michael Nicholson/Corbis.

Designer: Les Kanturek; Editor: Joann Jovinelly
Photo Researcher: Gabriel Caplan